Management Mentor: Techniques for New Managers

By Sean Donahoe

v 1.0

Dedication

I dedicate this book to my wife Jessica and my son Ian. Their love and support is what encourages me every day.

Acknowledgements

I'd like to acknowledge the support of my editor Heather LaForge in the creation of this book. Her judgment and guidance were critical to its success.

In addition, I'd like to acknowledge all those who have supported me in my management journey. In particular, I recognize the below managers from whom I've learned many of the enclosed techniques:

- Uzi Murad
- Dave Gerbitz
- Steve Sirich
- Lisa Utzschneider

Contents

1 - Welcome

I wrote this book in the summer of 2016 in
Britannia Beach, BC. The year prior to writing, I
had multiple management conversations with
several individuals. The conversations spanned
employees, mentees, friends, and family
members, but the topic was the same: How to
effectively lead as a new manager? It was as if
my personal and professional contacts had all
been promoted to managers in the same year.
The questions and concerns kept repeating
themselves. These were the exact same
questions I wrestled with when I moved into
management.

1. How do I hire strong people?
2. How can I get someone promoted?
3. How should I manage a lower performer?
4. Etc.

These questions arise because as individuals are
promoted to management they are often
provided no formal training. There is no
"Introduction to Managing People" course in
college. There is no MBA concentration in "First
Year Management". New managers are thrown
into their role with no formalized support. This
is a waste of talent.

true!

New managers are selected because they are
strong employees. Their companies bet on them
to play a larger part in the success of the firm.
However, these managers are then left to fend
for themselves. My friends, employees, etc. came

to me for guidance due to my personal success and passion for developing new managers. They were hungry for direction and guidance. They wanted to continue their professional success and were looking for mentorship to guide them in their new role.

Upon realizing this trend, I took several days to sequester myself and write down the most common management techniques for new managers. These techniques are by no means comprehensive. They represent the initial practices that a new manager should master in their first year.

Who I Am

I hold an Undergraduate Business Degree from Carnegie Mellon University and a Masters of Business Administration from Vanderbilt University. My work background spans consulting (American Management Systems), software telecommunications (Amdocs), and two large technology companies (Microsoft and Amazon). Throughout my career, I have learned various management practices, which are discussed throughout this book. Each chapter focuses on a core aspect of specific techniques that is applicable to a wide range of companies.

This book is written based on my personal background, culture, and experience. By its very nature, the text is biased in its approach. Before implementing the techniques outlined here, you should discuss them with your manager, mentor, peers, and Human Resource representative.

My Management Philosophy

One of the most difficult questions you will be asked as a manager is, what is your management philosophy? The question is similar to asking someone his or her religious affiliation. Are you Shia or Sunni? Are you Catholic, Evangelical, etc.? How you manage is deeply personal and is framed by your upbringing, company, and personality. To make the question even more complex, there are no clearly defined management styles. While there are titans of the management practice (Jack Welsh, W. Edward Demming, or Peter Drucker) individuals do not refer to themselves as Welshian or Drukerian in their management philosophy.

It will be up to you to construct your own philosophy or management religion. Here I present my core beliefs around management. The three philosophies outlined below are ideal for me but may not align with your own management philosophy:

1. Management is the art of extending your will. Effective managers stretch themselves beyond their immediate day-to-day engagement to extend their reach into their team. A manager's purpose is to drive his or her personal passion, goals, and values into their team. A manager should think of their team as a body. Each

part of the body is operating as individual parts in concert with one another. Overall the body is accomplishing what the mind desires. The mind extends its will across the body. Notice I did not write that a manager _imposes_ his or her will. You are not imposing your needs, desires, or goals onto your team. You are extending your will. You are managing people to perform what is required to reflect your will. As a manager, you want your team to act cohesively to move in the right direction. They may get there by different paths and they may use different skills than you, but they know without hesitation the direction you want them to go.

2. Management is relationships. A manager must understand effective professional relationships. As a new manager, you inherit a new type of relationship in your life. You have gone beyond a professional peer relationship into a new world of manager/employee relationship. One of the challenges of this relationship is that you have limited experiences to draw upon to understand the relationship. The media is full of various types of relationships (romantic, paternal, familial, friend, etc.) but rarely is the employee/manager relationship depicted, or if it is, it is often portrayed poorly (note: _Horrible Bosses,_

ro 'ghz' (circled)

Office Space, etc.). To make matters worse, you may have more employee relationships than family or friend relationships, and those employee relationships may all be given to you at once, as opposed to friendships, which are often made sequentially.

good point (handwritten note, right margin)

3. <u>Management requires accountability</u> As a manager, you must balance an additional level of accountability. You are accountable to the company, to your manager, your peers. But as a manager you are also accountable to your employees. <u>Managers must understand and balance those accountabilities, which are often in tension.</u> Your employee may want a day off, while the company needs someone to answer the phones. You need to understand what your accountabilities are to each of these stakeholders. Trading off these accountabilities can be difficult.

The three core tenets of my management philosophy (Extending your will, Relationships, Accountability) are how I approach managing people. As you develop as a manager you will likely develop your own approach. The techniques in this book will help you practice the basics of management as you develop your own personal philosophy.

What is Management Mentor?

Management Mentor is a company that develops managers and leaders. It was based on the belief that employees being promoted to management are wasted due to underinvestment in their professional development. Companies are selecting you for your ability to perform and then failing to support you in your new role. Our vision is for all managers and leaders to access to the tools and techniques they need to be successful.

Management mentor has three core principles:

1. Be Brave - As an organization focused on professional development, we believe that being brave is key to professional growth. Stepping beyond ourselves is how we grow both personally and professionally. As an organization, we take brave steps to push ourselves to what is possible.

2. Be Wise - We look to develop ourselves and others beyond rote knowledge. We strive to apply and evolve knowledge to become wisdom. Wisdom is the ability to know when and how to apply our knowledge. Management as a profession is a complex reality. Striving to be wise forces us to move beyond basic decision-making.

[handwritten margin notes: "thats how I feel about role this", "I like this"]

3. Be Trustworthy – We earn trust every day through the decisions and actions we take. To develop managers and leaders they must trust us, our process, and our content. We actively take steps to create moments of trust building, and limit trust breaking.

As individuals at Management Mentor, we seek to apply these three principles in our daily life. We ask ourselves each day. <u>How was I brave today? How was I wise</u> today? Did I act in a <u>trustworthy manner?</u>   *I need to be braver*

How to Use This Book

The techniques in this book will not benefit you if not applied practically. As with all new skills, practice leads to perfection. You will not perfect each technique the first time you perform it. To help with the implementation of these skills, each chapter is setup as follows:

1. Overview of skill – This section defines the heart of the skill. I describe what success looks like when practicing the technique; when the technique is used and, when applicable, a framework to use when performing the technique.

2. FAQs – This section includes a list of questions that you may have about the technique. They are specific in nature. The applicability of these questions depends

on your personality, culture, or business environment.

3. Accountability Questions– This section includes questions that should be asked of yourself twice: once immediately after reading the chapter, and then again after applying the technique. These questions are especially valuable if you are reading this book with a group of new managers or working through the book with a mentor. **The hardest thing will be to practice these techniques.** As a manager, you will have an overwhelming set of new expectations placed on you. **Make time to allow yourself to grow.**

To best use this book, I recommend tackling one chapter per month. Read the chapter, reflect on how you have practiced or seen the technique being practiced. During the month, look for ways to practice the technique. As a new manager, look for ways to engage others in the technique; as an individual looking to become a manager, watch how the technique is applied. At the end of the month, review the second FAQs per chapter for reflection.

What this book is not
This book is not a business degree. This book will not teach you accounting or finance. This book covers techniques that you are unlikely to gain in university or in your career before becoming a manager. This book is not the end of

becoming a manager. This book is the start; it is a guide for your journey. As previously mentioned, identifying a mentor for yourself is vital to your success as a manager. A mentor who understands your industry, professional culture, and company will help you apply the techniques in this book to your individual situation.

Additional Support
Reading this book will not be enough for you to master these techniques. Before moving forward, determine how you best learn. Is it by reading or talking, application versus reflection? Likely it is a combination of these. The reading of this book is only the starting point. You should set up a support network to ensure that you are practicing these techniques, and being held accountable to the practices recommended. Seek out people who you trust to help you as you work through your transition to manager. Some additional sources of support may be found in:

1. **Your manager** – This book can be used as a primer during weekly meetings with your manager. Take your first meeting of a month to review the chapter overview. How does your company practice this technique? How does your manager practice it? For the second meeting come with answers to the initial set of questions. Do your answers align with your

manager's? Finally, at the end of the month discuss how you have implemented the technique that month. What did you learn about yourself and the technique?

2. **A mentor** – As with your manager, a mentor can be a great accountability partner. You can use the same timeline as mentioned above with your mentor. Review the chapter with your mentor, practice the technique, then review what you learned.

3. **Peer Group** – Take the initiative and set up a peer group of new managers. You are all going through this transition together. You will have many of the same questions and concerns. A peer group allows you to bring up questions you may hesitate to broach with your manager.

4. **ManagementMentor.com** – ManagementMentor.com has many resources. Visit the site to download additional material, signup for a conference or connect with other managers.

The chapters do not have to be reviewed in order. There are certain times of the year when some chapters may be more relevant than others. Feel free to skip around throughout the year, to tie what is happening in your company with the techniques demonstrated.

Don't rush; plowing through the book without time to reflect and practice will limit your ability to grow and develop. To effectively work through the 15 technique chapters, plan to take between 15-18 months to complete the book.

how!

My hope is that at the end of this book you have the techniques to be a successful new manager.

2 - Setting a Vision

Teams perform best when they are aligned to and embrace a vision. A vision is a clear articulation of the end state of your business. A vision is different than mission, as they answer two separate questions. A mission answers the question: Why does your team matter? A vision answers: Where are we going?

A PC on every desktop. This was the vision set by Bill Gates in the early days of Microsoft. Amazon's vision is *to be Earth's most customer-centric company, where customers can find and discover anything they might want to buy online.* Each vision describes an end state for the business. While the end state of a business may never be realized, all employees will understand the direction to head. In this chapter, we will discuss how you can set and effectively communicate your team's vision.

What is a successful vision?
You know you have set a successful vision when you achieve buy-in from your management, your peers, and your team. A successful vision is one that all involved members understand and believe. You do not need everyone to think that the vision will ever be fully accomplished. You do, however, need buy-in that the direction towards the vision is the right path for your organization. If everyone believes your vision will be accomplished quickly and without any trouble, then your vision is likely not audacious

enough. Set a vision that is bold—one that is difficult to achieve but that excites your team.

A courageous vision will bring up fears or self-doubt. Work to quiet those questions by focusing on the direction that you are moving. As you present the vision to your team, there will be questions. Your team, partners, and even your manager will ask if the vision is feasible. That's ok! Wrestle through the questions. Doing so will instill passion in your team and an eagerness to follow your lead as you work down the path towards your vision. A clear vision aligns you, your team, your partners, and your manager to the direction your team will head.

When do you set a vision?
There are three times to set or reset a vision. The first is when you have a new team, the second when your vision has been accomplished, and finally if internal or external changes require you to change your vision.

When you create a new team one of the first things you should do is set a vision. Without a clear vision your team, partners, and manager won't know how to make decisions. This lack of clarity will lead to individuals working at cross-purposes. Within the first few days or weeks of a new team you should set a vision.

If your team has accomplished its vision, it's necessary to set a new one. Similar to a group that arrives at a destination, there will be questions of where to go next. Celebrate the accomplishment of the old vision, but be sure to set a new vision.

Don't be afraid to change your vision. Internal or external changes to your team may require a new vision. Perhaps the industry has evolved or perhaps your customer based has changed. Being too rigid in your vision may lead to your team the wrong direction. Conversely changing a vision taxes your team, so do so only when necessary. Balance the need to head in a consistent direction, with the evolution of your business.

How do you set a vision?
There are various ways to set a vision. The process of setting a vision primarily depends on the culture of your organization. Is it a bottom-up organization where team involvement is expected? Or is it a top down organization where managers make decisions and the team aligns to those decisions? Work with your manager to be sure you understand the cultural expectation of how visions are set in your company.

To craft an effective vision, begin by answering a few questions about your customer. Who is your customer? Are they internal or external? Do you need to constrain or expand your customer base? How do you talk about your current or future customers? Use language that your team will understand. After defining your customer, you must ask how will you make the customer's life better. How will their day be different? What aspect of their life will improve if your vision is accomplished? Get specific; imagine yourself as your customer in this end state. What are you doing? How does what you are doing differ from today?

Most visions have no end date. A vision is open ended and aspirational. Use language that drives an emotional response from your team. A vision is all about buy-in; your vision must take the employee into the future. Don't be wordy. A vision should be easy to memorize and recite. You want it embedded in everyday decision-making.

Be patient as you set your vision. It may take several weeks or months to finalize it. Try out multiple options. Why do you like one vision over another? Don't be afraid to iterate and refine. At some point, you must call it good. You may have anxiety in setting a vision that may never be accomplished. Don't fret! Visions change as you team evolves. Teams may never accomplish the vision. By setting a clear destination (even if not achievable) you align your team to work in concert as they move in the same direction.

How to communicate a vision
Once your vision is clear, it's time to get team members to buy-in. Use your business communication channels to drive the adoption of the vision. All hands meetings, 1:1s, posters, newsletters, goal updates, etc. are all strong options to promote your vision. Embed the vision

into your daily conversations. Remember the end state is a vision that is used in day-to-day decision-making. To achieve that end state, you want the vision internalized by the team.

Remember to follow up to be sure that your vision has been successfully adopted into your work culture. Check with your team members several weeks after setting the vision. Have they internalized the vision? Can they repeat it? Most importantly, are decisions being made that will move your team towards the vision? Know how to measure progress and reward your team as they move towards the vision in their daily work.

FAQs

1. My team needs several visions, what do I do?

When a manager asks this question, it may mean they don't understand the underlying path that their team is on. What about your team unifies them? Do they work on the same product? Do they work for the same customer? You may need to take a step back and set one clear vision for your team, otherwise you lose the cohesion necessary for progress.

There may be times when you manage two or three truly separate teams. In that case, it is ok to have a vision for each team. In this situation, it is necessary to think of them as separate teams. A team cannot be unified if it has multiple visions.

2. My broader group has a vision; do I need an additional vision?

If the broader group's vision is used in your daily decision-making, it may be perfect for your team. Often new managers are managing smaller teams that exist within a larger group; in that case, there may be no need for a separate vision. However, if you are part of a larger group and that larger group doesn't have a vision, work with your manager to decide if you should create a vision for your individual team or if your manager will create a vision for the broader group.

3. I can't get my manager/peer/team to buy into my vision. They don't understand where I want to take them.

First ask yourself: What is causing the resistance? The problem may be the articulation of the vision. Have you laid out the vision in language that is emotionally inspiring? Have you used too many technical words? Are you being too vague? Does it paint a word picture in their minds?

If you have communicated your vision properly, you must ask why your team doesn't want to follow it. Are they afraid of the journey? Or do they believe the destination is the wrong one? If they are afraid of the journey, it's time to put on your leadership hat and inspire them. While the journey may be difficult, it will be worth the pay off. If they disagree with the end state, ask yourself what information do they have that you don't? Are they making different assumptions than you are? Try to drill down to the specific areas where there is disagreement. Then look for ways to respond to it. Go out and capture additional data. Survey your customers. Take the vision to executive leadership to get feedback. In the end, if you have set a vision that your team won't follow, you are walking a path alone. You must ensure buy-in, so take the time to sort through these questions to unify your team.

Questions after reading the chapter
1. Does your team already have a vision? Is it the correct vision?
2. What is your company's vision? Have you memorized it?
3. What gets your creative juices flowing? How can you create an environment where you can envision yourself in your customer's shoes?

Questions after setting a vision
1. What's your vision? Don't peek; just say it out loud. If you haven't memorized it, ask yourself: is it truly memorable?

2. What decisions have you made using your vision? Did you decide anything differently this week by setting a clear vision?

3. At the end of your meetings this week, ask someone to repeat your vision. Has your team memorized it? Can your partners recite the key aspects of your vision?

4. How have you embedded your vision into your work space? Have you set up posters, stickers, awards, etc. Does each employee see your vision every day when they come to work?

3 - Goal Setting

The ability to effectively set business goals is an often-overlooked skill of a manager. Goals serve multiple purposes for a team. First, goals determine success. A manager measures success by answering these questions: Where is the goal line for the person, project, or team? How will we know when we have reached the end state? Second, goals help manage performance. By setting goals, team members will know how they have met their objectives and against which bar to measure themselves. Finally, goals help partners hold *your team* accountable, while giving them an understanding of what *you* will accomplish by when. This clarity affords your partners the opportunity to align their goals with yours.

What is success?

Successful goals often use the S.M.A.R.T. framework. There have been various words tied to each letter for this framework. Below is the acronym I have found to be the most fruitful for me.

S – Specific – A goal is specific when there is one concept contained within. Often managers will struggle with setting goals that encapsulate a single concept. It can be difficult to simplify your business down to a few specific goals. Lack of specificity can be a result of a vague or undefined vision.

M - Measurability – Can you measure the goal? What metrics exist or need to be built so you can effectively measure the goal? Without knowing where the finish line is how can you complete the goal? It should be clear to anyone who reads the goal how to determine when it is accomplished. Does everyone involved with the goal understand how it will be measured?

A – Actionable – Can this goal be acted upon? Are you waiting for other partners, or resources to act? No one wants a goal that they cannot accomplish. A goal is actionable if you (and your team) understand how to move forward to accomplish the goal. The full plan to accomplish the goal may not be known, but everyone must understand which direction to start heading to begin to accomplish it.

R – Realistic – Realistic does not mean easy. Realistic means that the accomplishment of the goal is within the boundary of the possible. Often this is the most difficult part of goal setting. When goals are used (as they often are) to evaluate the performance of an employee, team members may consciously or subconsciously choose goals that are easy to accomplish. Conversely, some companies focus on setting goals that are overly aggressive or audacious, which may be discouraging to employees.

The likelihood of accomplishing a goal should be based on your company's culture and the state of your team. In some companies, failing to meet a goal may result in immediate termination. Others may expect that only 50% of goals will be met. In those environments, achievements above 50% will lead to questions about how aggressive the goals were when set. The health of the team will determine the how aggressive a goal should be set. A team that has gone through a significant change may require easier goals than a high performing team.

T – Time bound – Goals (as opposed to visions) should be time bound. Setting a clear date for goal accomplishment aligns the team. Ideally the timeframe of the goal balances the effort required to accomplish the goal and the business need. Sometimes external factors drive a goal date. For example, in a retail environment you may want a project completed before the holiday season begins. Regulations may require compliance by a certain date. Don't be afraid to set arbitrary goal dates to drive a sense of urgency.

When do you set goals?

Goals can be set on various time frames. At the companies, I have worked for there are usually three goal setting cycles. The first cycle for goal setting is **annual**. This cycle is particularly important because the business world often looks at performance on an annual basis. Additionally, by setting goals on an annual basis you align to annual reviews and financial reporting. The next cycle is **quarterly or monthly**. Certain industries or teams may evolve at a pace that does not allow for annual goal setting. In that case, setting goals on a quarterly or monthly basis may be more effective. Finally, **daily or weekly** goals may be set. Recent concepts such as Kanban or Scrum are designed to set goals at a daily or weekly basis. This allows for rapid delegation of resources and prioritization.

Companies often set goals on all these timelines. Having big annual goals that flow into monthly goals, which then flow into daily goals, can effectively balance speed and consistency.

How to set goals

The setting of effective goals is a process. Managers often under-invest time needed to set goals. Goals are one of the most powerful ways to drive your business. Investing time in the crafting of your goals will pay off in the long run. This section describes the setting of goals on an annual basis. Similar methodology can be applied to Quarterly/Monthly/Weekly/Daily goal setting, but with an accelerated time frame.

Before writing a goal, review where your business is and where you want it to be:

- Review your vision – Take a moment to review your mission and vision. Where is your business and team heading? Why does your team exist?

- Review your key business metrics – What numbers define your business? Revenue, costs, etc.. These key business metrics can help you in your measurement of goals.
- External/Internal Pressures – What changes are happening in the industry? What changes are happening internally? How do those pressures impact your team?
- Where do you want to be? – Where is the end state in the next 12 months? Similar to the vision of your team, a clear picture of where you want to be in 12 months is critical to goal setting.
- What needs to change to get there? – What are the primary levers needed to move your business towards that end state. Where should you invest? Where should you stop investing?
- Resources – What resources do you have? What resources can you get?
- Team Feedback – In your next 1:1s capture feedback on the both goal setting process and proposed goals. What worked in the goal setting process last year? What needs to change? Team members who understand how to influence goals will feel more accountable to goals. Ask your team members the above questions. Where do they think the industry is going?

What is the most important thing the team can accomplish?

Now that you have an overview of where you are as a business, it is time to set goals. A simple way to set a goal is to use a declarative sentence.

A will accomplish B by C date.

A – This is the person that is responsible for the goal. Single threaded ownership is important to drive accountability. While many teams or partners may work on a goal, having an explicit owner of the goal is critical. Someone must feel uniquely accountable for the success/failure of accomplishing a goal.

B – The heart of the goal. This can be thought of as deliverable or a metric. In a deliverable goal, for example "launch feature x", it is important to define what is included in feature x. This may require a supplemental documentation that describes the feature.

C – The date of the goal. This may also be a specific time for daily goals. Bob will accomplish project xyz by 5pm.

Metric Setting
Metric goals are measured in two ways. Explicit measurement (for example, "Deliver revenue of $100") is the clearest way to define a goal. A second way is to look at changes in a metric. For example, Improve revenue by 10%. Each

organization may have a preferred way to measure goals.

An important aspect of metrics is clarity on the definition of the metric. A document that defines each metric may be required to define exactly how a metric will be captured. This is often the most difficult component of finalizing a metric-based goal. Getting into the details of what is in or out of a metric is an important detail to understand and communicate.

Iteration and Buy in of Goals

Once you have an initial draft of goals, you should begin iterating and securing commitment from your team, manager, and partners. Hold several reviews with your team. Doing so will allow your team to bring up additional goals or communicate a desire to remove some goals. Use these sessions to gauge buy in on the goals. What is the team's spoken and unspoken reaction to the proposed goals? Do the goals make the team excited? Nervous? Understanding those reactions is critical to attain buy in from your team on the goals themselves. Providing multiple channels (1:1s, Team Meetings, Email, etc.) to capture feedback is important, as individuals process and communicate feelings on and reaction to goals in various ways. Listen to their feedback; gauge their reaction.

You should work with your partner teams to drive alignment of goals. Be prepared to get into the details (or the supplemental documents) of the goals. Understand how your goals overlap and align with your partners' goals. Do you need to give a goal to another team? Do you need to take on a goal from a partner team? What resources are required for the various teams to meet your goals? Do you need resources from other teams to accomplish the goals they have for your team?

After several iterations and reviews it is important to draw a line when goals are finalized. Though goals may be updated or changed, it is necessary to have a starting line for annual goals. This is important from a performance management standpoint, as individuals want to understand where their performance review starts and ends. Goals that are aligned to the same time frame as when individuals are reviewed helps in performance management. Individuals do not want to be evaluated against goals that are finalized 6 months into the act of accomplishing the goal.

FAQs
1. When should I update my goals?
   Goals should be updated when they are no longer serving their purpose of driving the business. If a goal is unattainable within a given time frame it must be revised. If the goal is vague it must be updated. If the

business or industry has changed direction, the goal must be changed. Each company has unique cultural expectations on when and how to change a goal. Speak with your manager if you believe a goal should be updated.

2. How do I address sequential goals?
   Sequential goals are ones where the desired end state requires multiple goals to be accomplished. We must do A, then B, then C. You should decide if A, B, and C are tasks or goals. A goal is one in which you will spend significant effort to accomplish. A task can be delivered quickly and is easily understood as a component of a broader goal. You may choose to make A, B, and C goals in addition to an overall goal. Therefore, you can track progress on A, B, and C as your team works towards the final goal.

3. At what level should I set goals?
   Goals should be set at all levels of the organization. Your employees should have goals, which then roll into your goals, which roll into your manager's, etc.

4. How many goals should I have?
   Goals should reflect the entirety of your business. If you have employees working on something not tied to a goal, decide if they should be working on that, and if so

create a goal. Another constraint is to consider the effort to report out on goals. If you have 100s of goals it will take 100s of minutes to report out on them. Balance the need for precision in your goals with the cost it takes to track and update goals. My new managers will have between 5 and 20 annual goals.

Questions after reading the chapter

1. Do you know your goals? How are they different than when you were an individual contributor?
2. What was the last goal you accomplished? Was it clear when you accomplished it? What metric showed that you met the goal?
3. What are your manager's goals? Do they align to your goals?

Questions after your first goal setting

1. Do your goals encompass everything that your team is doing? What percentage of your team's time is spent on goals? What time is unaccounted for?
2. Are all your goals S.M.A.R.T.?
3. What aspect of the goal setting was the most difficult? Where do you need to improve?
4. How many goals did you set? How many does each team member have?

4 - Hiring

The attraction, evaluation, and closing of new employees provide never-ending tasks for a manager. Having a structured approach to hiring will set you up for success.

What is Success?

Effective hiring is critical to your business. Your ability to bring in talent for your team will enable you to be successful over the long term. Successful hiring can be measured by two goals: Efficiency and Quality. To measure efficiency, you need to ask yourself: How efficient are you with your and your team's time in hiring? How many hours of recruiting time does it take you, your team, and your recruiters to hire an employee? To determine the quality of your hiring process, ask yourself the following: What is the 1-year retention and performance of the employees your hire? Are you bringing in talent that thrives or struggles in your roles? Efficiency and Quality are critical metrics for hiring success.

Hiring is an ongoing process. Even if you currently have no open headcount, maintaining your network is important. Keep track of where potential talent is going. What firms are attracting people? What firms are teams leaving? Maintaining your network even when you are not actively hiring will pay off in the long run.

What are effective hiring techniques?

Training/Policies

Before starting a hiring process, you should ensure that the individuals involved in the hiring process (recruiters, interviewers, etc.) have taken all appropriate trainings. Each locale will have various laws around what is acceptable and not acceptable in an interviewing process. In addition, your company will have its own process and hiring requirements that you must understand. Interviewing alone encompasses several logistics that may vary from company to company. Do you need hands-on training on the tool used for tracking interviews? Who sets up the phone screens? Who books a room? Who meets the candidate to get them into the building, etc.? An effective recruiting process is full of tiny details. The more specifics you understand of your company's process, the better.

Job Description

Once you have reviewed your company's policies and processes, the next step in hiring is to create a job description. The job description notifies potential candidates what the role will entail. There are usually five sections to a job description. They are:

1. The Hook – In the first 2-3 sentences appeal to why the candidate should keep reading. As in effective advertising, you

need a quick appeal to spark interest in the candidate.

2. The Overview – The next 3-8 sentences should provide broad context of the role. If you were explaining the position to someone in your industry, how would you describe the role? The answer to this question provides the overview.

3. The Goals – What goals will this employee be tasked with? If you filled this role today, what would you expect the individual to accomplish?

4. The Skills – What skills are required for this position? Skills should be classified as technical (programming skills, accounting, etc.) and interpersonal. (Bias for Action, Interpersonal Awareness, Influence without Authority) etc.

5. Minimum Requirements –These would be the requirements that the individual must have. By stating these as the minimum you are agreeing that you will not hire anyone without these skills. Be extra cautious when setting these requirements.

After you have written the job description share it with to your manager, your peers, and your employees. Ask for their feedback. Does the job description match what they believe the role entails? By shopping the job description around you will improve the description and embed a seed with these individuals about the opening. In upcoming 1:1s your manager, peers, or employees may remember your open job and pass along candidates to you.

Finally, review the job description with your recruiter. Because of their expertise, they will have seen significantly more job descriptions (and candidates) than you have. Utilize their background and knowledge to update and refine your job description.

Network

Once you have finished your job description and posted it through your recruiting tool you should activate your professional network. A network can be thoughts of as a series of concentric circles:

1. Inner Circle – Immediate co-workers, friends, family – These are people you work with closely or interact with frequently. You know their strengths and weaknesses directly. If you felt that they were right for the role you would approach them directly about the role. Inner circles are crucial in broadcasting your needs to our middle circle. Make sure your inner circle has the job description easily available and are discussing it in their day-to-day interactions.

2. Middle Circle – Business Contacts – This middle circle is the most effective connection for hiring. These are people in your network that at one point you have worked with but are not currently. The

volume of these contacts is often high, and they are not necessarily at the forefront of your mind when you first open the role because they are outside of your day-to-day interactions. However, this circle is precisely the one you need to be the most diligent about maintaining. A quick email to or coffee with high performers in this circle when you aren't hiring keeps the relationship warm for when you begin to hire. This is also the circle where your former mentors and mentees sit. Mentors and mentees are a great source of leads. Individuals that have you have invested in or who have invested in you provide an excellent group of candidates.

3. Outer Circle – Contact of Contact – These individuals are those with whom you do not have direct contact. These are contacts that come from your network. To activate these contacts, post your job description on broad networks such as Facebook or LinkedIn. These tools will allow your post to be shared beyond your immediate contacts into a broader network. These individuals do not know you, so the success rate of these posts will be low.

Recruiters & Agencies
In addition to your network you should be working with your recruiter or an external agency. Recruiters and agencies are paid to mine

the vast pool of potential candidates. The way to effectively work with recruiters is to align on your goals of efficiency and quality. How fast can an agency get a role filled? What is the quality of the candidates provided by the agency? Failures in working with recruiters or agencies are often the fault of the hiring manager who are unable to precisely describe the ideal candidate. When working with recruiters and agencies it is important that you do your part to keep the open role at the forefront of their mind. Weekly meetings, lunch, a casual swing by their desk, are all ways to ensure the recruiter and agency remember your position.

Be sure you also work closely with your recruiter on the logistics of the interview itself. Who does the scheduling, who books the room, who arranges for lunch, badge access, etc.? Often new managers run into problems on the day of the interview due to not walking through these details with their recruiter.

Interviewing Process
The interview process is expensive for both the candidate and the company. Count the hours both sides spend on the interview process; it can easily exceed 100 hours to complete an interview process. With such an investment in time you would think there would be better understanding of what makes an effective interview. Interviewing processes are like fads; different industries or different decades will have various models of interviewing. Meeting with

your recruiter and fully immersing yourself in how your firm conducts interviews is critical. If possible, ask to shadow some of the most successful interviewers, and then meet with them to ask questions. Ask why they picked question x or y. How did they interpret answer a or b?

Evaluating a candidate will be very difficult within a given hour (or even 2 hours). To best utilize the allotted time, you should identify what skills and experiences are critical for this role. Once you have identified those skills and experiences, slot them into the various interviews the candidate will go through. For example, what do you want to discern during the initial phone screen? What are you looking to identify at phone screen two, etc.? The allocation of skills should be designed to screen out early on those skills that a candidate may not meet. If you are hiring for a software engineer and you need a specific skill, don't wait till the 4th interview to test for that skill; use the first interview to weed out those who will not be able to perform. On the other hand, if most candidates perform well on communication skills leave that interview for later in the process.

The goal of an interview is to maximize your confidence that the candidate can perform the specific skills required for the role. This is a simple statement but it can be difficult to execute.

Let's break down this goal. We will begin with the phrase, "maximize your confidence". At the end of the day you need to ether hire or not hire each candidate. Therefore, the interview process must provide you with as much information as possible for you to make that decision. Every minute of the interview should be focused on providing you with actionable information to ensure that you are confident in your decision.

"perform the skill." Don't get muddled here. Remain focused on the specific skill for which you are interviewing. Others on the interview loop will focus on their areas of expertise; you must trust their judgment to allow sufficient time in the interview to spend evaluating each necessary skill.

"required for the role." Ensure that you (and your interviewers) understand the level from each skill you expect from this position. Often interviewers will want to compare a candidate to an existing employee or another candidate; resist this temptation. In your mind construct a mythical ideal candidate. This candidate meets all the skills required for this role. Keeping in mind the level required will allow you to mentally evaluate the real-life candidate, against this ideal candidate.

There are various frameworks to increase your confidence around whether or not to hire an individual. I will describe two frameworks.

Behavioral Interviewing Framework – This framework is often described as "best predictor of future behavior is past behavior". In this framework, you are looking for specific examples of the employee's <u>behavior</u> to identify how they will act in future situations. If you were to evaluate someone's behavior in a situation think about what information you would want to know before judging their behavior.

1. Situation – What is the situation? For a given behavior you want to understand ask about a situation that highlights that behavior. For example, if you wanted to understand how an employee builds trust, ask for a situation about building trust with another team.

2. Action – What was the action or decision the employee choose to make? Did they do x or y? Often a follow-up question can be good here. For example, in the trust building example questions such as: Why did you take that action to improve trust? If you had to do it again would you do the same action?

3. Result – Was the action successful? Did the outcome match your expectations?

As you build a list of behavioral questions it's important to remember your goal of deciding to hire or not hire. You want questions that provide you information to make that decision. If all

Good point!

candidates fail your question or if all candidates pass your question, then the question does not help you decide. You want questions that only those candidates that can be successful at the role pass the question.

Case Interviewing Framework – A case interviewing process is designed to "determine how a candidate problem solves". As such, the case framework should only be used in those situations where the role will require on your feet problem solving. The problem with the case framework is that it is relatively rare for employees to be put in a daily situation where the must be constantly thinking on their feet. If you believe you have a role that requires this skill, then the case framework can be useful in filtering out candidates. For example, a policeman is often thinking on their feet. There are many books on case questions. I prefer to use questions that mirror a real-life situation on the team. Again, remember to choose case questions that not all candidates pass or fail. You want answers that help you screen.

Other – There are other frameworks that can be used (Brain teasers, group interviews, etc.). Feel free to try alternatives, but hold firm to the bar that the interview must increase your confidence in a hire/no hire decision. Track and validate the framework you use to ensure you end up with quality candidates. Don't be afraid to review the interview approach of your company and ask for an in-depth analysis of the success of the

interesting way to phrase it

process. The science of interviewing in 2017 has not emerged with a clear winner.

Debrief

After the interviews have finished it is helpful to meet as a group to discuss the feedback. As a hiring manager, you will have a conscious (or unconscious) desire to have your role filled. You will tend to compromise to meet your current need. Do not do it! The tax of hiring an individual below your needs will cost you in time and effort. Many firms will have a secondary hiring manager that is hiring on behalf of the firm and not your team. While at first glance it may seem frustrating, this sets up a healthy tension between yourself and this secondary hiring manager. Utilize this balance to your benefit.

At the debrief everyone will present his or her feedback. The purpose of the conversation among those present is to improve your confidence in a hire/no hire decision. Ask probing questions to improve your confidence. Ask interviewers for their level of confidence. If they are not confident in a candidate, ask why? What is preventing that confidence? Was it the candidate's lack of interviewing skills or was it something about his or her professional skills. Teasing apart this difference is crucial. When someone says, "there was just something about this candidate...." jump on that comment and hold them accountable for providing confidence to your decision.

At the end of the debrief, you must land on a
decision whether to make an offer. A double yes
is the hurdle. Both you and the company hiring
manager must agree to move ahead. A no hire
vote from either of you is a no hire.

very Amazon

Offer Process

Each company will have various ways of
presenting and negotiating an offer. The more
process oriented and the less human judgment
involved the better. Hopefully your firm will be
making 100s if not 1,000s of offers a year. The
more programmatic this process is, the less risk
of errors. Work with your HR representative to
understand the process at your firm and dive
into the details. While you may or may not be the
one handling the negotiation, an in-depth
understanding of the complete package (salary,
bonus, benefits, stock, etc.) is critical. As a
manager, you are accountable for how your
employees are paid and you must know the
details of each package.

I appreciate that!

Recruiting Metrics

Periodically sit with your recruiter and review
your goals on efficiency and quality. Regarding
efficiency, ask yourself, how many hours does it
take for you to hire a candidate? Are those hours
increasing or decreasing? Does it vary by role or
level? What step in the process is taking up a lot
of time with little return? Are you passing 99% of
all your candidates to 2nd phone screen? If so,
should you eliminate the first phone screen? Or

should you change the questions for that initial screen?

Regarding quality, take time to investigate those employees you have hired. Compare their first review to the interview feedback. Are there patterns that are being missed? Are your employees all getting a pass in communication during the interview, but then underperforming in that area once they are hired? Your goal should be that the quality of new hires remains high with few employees being managed out. You want the risks identified in the interview to match the gaps identified in their review. Effective interviews will identify the risks in a candidate that manifest themselves in the first year.

Question Evaluation
Reusing your questions is an important skill. By using the same question time and time again you can refine and determine the effectiveness of the question in increasing your confidence. Rate your questions after every 25 interviews. Which question increases your confidence in the hire/no hire decision? Which question does not add much value? Be ruthless in the utilization of questions. Remember the goal: You must maximize your confidence in whether to hire a candidate.

FAQ

1. How do you find effective questions to ask
   interviewees?
   Often your firm will have a pool of
   questions for the most common skills and
   values. Take initiative and begin tracking
   questions across your team. Ask each
   interviewer to add in new question each ℞
   month. Have them rate the question on
   how effective it is in deciding to hire or not
   hire.

2. Should I have a written test before I hold
   interviews?
   In some roles, a written test can be very
   effective. Be wary, however, of kicking out
   too many candidates based on the written
   test alone. Take a subset of candidates
   that did not pass and send them through
   your interview process. Did the test
   effectively determine how they did at the
   interview? In addition, be aware that
   written tests can be leaked. In a prior role I
   had, we were using a written test and it
   had been posted online. Fortunately for us
   (unfortunately for the candidates) the
   answers that were leaked were incorrect.
   We always knew which candidate had
   cheated and used the power of the
   Internet to answer our quiz.

   how!

3. Should I do group interviews?
   Think about the role you want to fill. If the
   role is one that will require a commanding
   presence in new situations, then a group

interview can work well. However, if you need someone to sit and work solo for hours on end, a group interview may not be the most effective. Look at all interview techniques in the framework of efficiency and quality. Group interviews can be very efficient, but they may not provide you with quality candidates.

4. How often should I reach out to my network?

The frequency with which you reach out to your network depends on the quality of the individual and the likelihood you will need their skills. If there are candidates that I believe are exceptional performers and hold skills in roles I frequently hire, I will meet with them quarterly for coffee, an after-work drink, or maybe send them a quick email. For individuals that are strong performers, but in a different industry or role than I require, I may contact them annually. Some individuals I just passively watch on LinkedIn. What roles they are in? What jobs have they posted?

5. Should I use xxxx? (Dice, Monster, LinkedIn, etc.)

Again, look back at your key metrics. Are these channels effective in terms of volume of candidates per hour invested in them? Do they produce quality candidates? Recently I have focused exclusively on LinkedIn, but I have used various services in the past. Work with your recruiter, and

see if you can pull metrics for the past 6
months across your company, and
determine what service has resulted in the
most hires per hour spent.

Questions to review after reading the chapter

1. Does your recruiter have metrics on
   efficiency and quality? Can you pull them
   yourself? Even an estimate will help you
   get started. How many hours does it take
   to hire a candidate? What has been your
   success rate of the candidates your group
   has hired in the past year?

2. Do you have a standard list of questions
   you use per value or skill? If they are not
   being documented, start writing them
   down now. What were the questions you
   used in your last interview? Did they help
   you decide?

3. What subconscious traits of candidates
   may you be biased for or against? We all
   have subconscious cultural biases. What
   mechanism does your firm have in place to
   mitigate these biases? Are you
   subconsciously eliminating candidate
   based on aspects that are not relevant to
   the business?

4. Do you know the details of a candidates
   interviewing experience? Who sets up the
   room? Who pays for lunch? How are they
   reimbursed for their travel? Candidates
   have very little information to base their
   decision to join a firm. Candidates will

49

extrapolate from seemingly minor details big themes about your company. Make those details work for you vs. against you.

Questions to review after your first hire

1. What was your level of confidence when you decided to hire the candidate? 100%? 75%? 50%? What steps are you taking to improve your confidence? What specific question will you ask in the future that you didn't ask previously? What will you have your interview team do differently?

2. What were the details of the offer? Do you understand the offer package? Can you explain it to a new hire on the first day that they join?

3. Were there candidates you did not hire? Are you tracking why you didn't hire them? If there are patterns, how can you move the identification of those gaps earlier in the process?

4. Go back and review your metrics. How many hours did it take to hire this candidate? After a year, verify if the risks identified in the interview process showed in their review.

5 - Onboarding a Team Member

The start of any new job is a big change for anyone. As a manager, it is important for you to ensure your employee has a successful transition to their new role. The faster an employee ramps into a new role, the quicker they will be in adding value to your team. A manager that addresses an employee's fears and concerns will be on their way to building a healthy relationship with their employee.

Onboarding to a new role generates questions and concerns. As a manager, you will determine the various ways a new employee can get answers to their questions and concerns. Remember that employees each have unique learning styles. Cultural and personal norms vary from employee to employee, so having multiple paths to get answers to questions is critical.

What is a successful onboarding?

A successful onboarding occurs when an employee is a fully productive member of your team. The level of complexity of the role will set the timing from start date to fully productive team member. For some roles, a few hours maybe all that is required, for others it may take months.

Setting clear goals for the role, and a clarity on what type of information the employee should know is important. By defining goals and what an employee must learn allows both you and your employee to set a point in time when they are to be fully productive. It's important to document this end date so expectations on both sides of the relationship are clear.

When do you onboard a team member?

When a new employee is hired, you need to onboard them. However, managers forget about onboarding internal transfers or even inter-team transfers. Moving to a new role with a company opens some of the same questions and concerns as starting in a new company. Don't forget to have a plan to onboard internal employees.

How do you do onboard a team member?

To effectively onboard a team member, you need a plan. You should create a written plan and review it in your 1:1s weekly with the new team member. The plan should have explicit items for the new employee to perform, and resources for them to use to achieve their role. A sample outline of an onboarding plan is as follows:

1. Welcome Message
2. Company/Team Overview
   a. Mission Statement – Why does this company and team exist?
   b. Vision Statement - Where is this company and team going?
   c. Company Values – What values does this company and team follow?
   d. Goals – What are the company and team goals?

    e. Team Structure – Where does the employee fit within the team and the company?

3. Role Description
   a. Job Description – What role did the employee accept?
   b. Short Term Goals –What do you expect of them as they onboard?
   c. Long Term Goals – What are the goals for this role once they are fully onboarded?

4. Pay/Benefits
   a. Pay – How much and when is an employee paid?
   b. Benefits – Overview of company benefits. Include resources for employee to learn more.

5. Policies
   a. Employee Handbook – Where is the employee handbook?
   b. HR – How does one contact HR?
   c. Travel & Entertainment and Expense – What are the policies around spending money on the company's behalf? How is the employee reimbursed for these expenses?

6. Work Environment
   a. Safety – What safety related information is provided?
   b. Physical Aspects – Where is their desk, chair, office, etc.?

      c. Work Time – What are requirements/norms for when the employee will be at work?

      d. Contact information – How can the employee contact you, peers, etc.?

7. Technology

      a. Email – How do they log in? What are Email norms?

      b. Email Lists – What are the appropriate email lists (Distribution Lists) the employee should join?

      c. Instant Messaging – What instant messaging tools are used?

      d. Websites & Wikis – Where, when, and how is information documented? What should the employee read to get up to speed on information related to their role?

      e. Applications – What applications should the employee have access to? How do they get access?

8. Trainings

      a. In Person – What trainings are required in person?

      b. Online – What trainings are required online?

      c. Optional – What trainings are considered required vs. optional?

9. Partners/Buddies

      a. Onboarding Names/Contacts – Who should the employee be meeting with during their onboarding phase?

b. Ongoing Names/Contacts – Provide a subset of the onboarding names/contacts. These are individuals the employee will meet with once they are ramped.

10.   Mentors

a. Onboarding Mentor – Provide the name of an individual who is typically a peer of the new employee. The onboarding mentor acts as the first point of escalation for questions during the onboarding phase. Where's the bathroom? Where's document xxx? Etc.

b. Culture Mentor – Providing an employee a mentor is critical, as the mentor will give them a different POV than you will as their manager. Having a dedicated mentor outside of the team gives the employee an additional perspective about the company. This relationship should be focused on guiding the new employee through the culture of the company. What does its mission, vision, values mean in everyday work? How are they applied day to day?

11.   You

a. What is your management philosophy?

b. What are your expectations of the employee/manager relationship?

c. How is it best to communicate with you?
d. What are your pet peeves?

Tracking Onboarding Progress?

Periodic check-ins with the new employee are critical to ensuring the onboarding process is progressing as planned. Many managers fail to invest enough time in new employees and thus slow the onboarding process. Consider adjusting your personal schedule to find additional time to spend with your new employee. Weekly check-ins are a minimum and more often meeting two or three times a week is more appropriate. By having frequent check-ins, you will be able to quickly course correct against the plan.

FAQs

1. How do I find an onboarding buddy or a mentor?

   Folks are often pleased to be asked to mentor someone. By asking, you show that you view them as a fully capable employee with information to share. Send a short email in which you describe the candidate, the role, your expectations of them, and the time expected for the current employee. Reminder this is a request and not a requirement. Due to other goals, business expectations an individual may not be able to spend time for a new mentee. For an onboarding buddy it may be two, ten minute chats a day for 3-4 weeks. For a mentor, it may be 30 minutes every other week for 4 months.

2. How long should it take to onboard someone?

   This varies dramatically based on the individual and the role. What are the complexities in the role? How nuanced is your firm's decision making? Are things formally documented or will the employee have to hunt around to get questions answered. Ask your peer mentors how long it takes them to onboard employees.

3. They took the training, why are they still making mistakes?

   Professional learning is different than learning in school. As you age, the brain is less flexible and is out of practice in learning. Meet with your employee, how do they best learn? What aspect are the struggling with? Have you provided more than one way to learn the task? For example, have you offered formal training, buddies, written procedures, videos, etc.? How long did it take other employees to learn the task? Offer the benefit of the doubt, but don't let an underperforming employee drift along. You must set a clear date when they be evaluated as a typical employee. Set a date for onboarding to end and they should be fully ramped.

Questions to review after reading the chapter

1. Think back to when you started with the company. What went well and what didn't? What do you wish someone had told you the first week?
2. Does your team or company have an onboarding template? Is it effective? What would make it better?
3. What logistical details are always forgotten for new employees? Do they never have a laptop the first day? What about access to systems? Often companies get 90% of the logistics correct but consistently fail on the same 10%. How can you ensure that doesn't happen?

Questions to review after your first employee has been onboarded

1. How fast did it take for your employee to be fully onboarded? Was it longer or shorter than you expected?
2. Did you review the onboarding document with the new employee? What part did they use the most? What part did they not use? What would they add now that they are onboarded?
3. How do you maintain this document? How do you scale it? How can you share it with other managers? Can you work on a template that contains 90% of the same content?

4. Have you finalized your new employee's goals? Have you reviewed your company values with them?

6- Defining the Employee & Manager Relationship

To establish how you will relate to your
employees (and vice versa) you must create an
effective definition for the employee/manager
relationship. Your ability to frame the
relationship will set expectations for both
parties. The below framework is based on an at-
will, high tech, American cultural perspective. As
in many aspects of management, your cultural
background, your company policies, and your
personal experiences will determine your
personal framing of the relationship.

What is Success?

A successful employee/manager relationship in
one that is mutually beneficial to both parties.
Both individuals have roles to play within the
context of the work environment. Within at-will
employment organizations, either party may
choose to exit the relationship at any time. By
defining and executing what each party desires
from the relationship, you will create a
productive working relationship.

When do you do it?

It is important to define expectations of both
parties early in the relationship. Take a few
minutes to discuss the relationship as part of the
onboarding of a new employee and then
periodically with existing employees.

How do you do it?

There are many ways of addressing a professional employee/manager relationship. I utilize the model that defines the relationship as a third entity. There is the employee, the manager, and the relationship. It can be beneficial to see the relationship as separate from the individuals (you and the employee).

Defining ownership of the relationship is important. Both parties are 50/50 owners in the relationship. Neither party fully controls the relationship and neither is fully responsible for the relationship. By defining co-ownership both the manager and the employee are jointly invested in its success and failure. Co-ownership also reduces the bias for control or passivity in the relationship. People bring their own personalities and backgrounds into any relationship. Some may choose to aggressively work to define and own the relationship fully. They will want to control all agendas, all discussion points, and focus the relationship on solving only their concerns. On the flip side, some employees may feel like ownership of the relationship is the sole responsibility of the manager. This can cause them to be a passive partner in the relationship, and in extreme cases may create a feeling of victimhood or lack of control of their working situation. A 50/50 split ownership provides both you and your employee a stake in the success or failure of the relationship.

6- Defining the Employee & Manager Relationship

Once you have identified how you will frame the relationship, you must determine what you and your employee desire for the relationship. What are you and your employee looking from the relationship? Employees are individuals and will differ in what they want out of you as a manager. These needs may vary by year, month, or daily. Being explicit in what needs you will and will not fulfill will minimize concerns on both sides of the relationship. Below is a sample list of employee needs:

1. Direction – The employee needs a manager to tell them to X or Y.
2. Prioritization – The employee wants a manager to help prioritize their tasks.
3. Coaching – The employee wants the manager to come alongside them.
4. Accountability – The employee needs the manager to hold them accountable for their performance.
5. Training – The employee wants the manager to teach them.
6. Wisdom – The employee wants the manager to teach them more than just skills, but also a deeper wisdom of the position, industry, or technologies.
7. Motivation – The employee wants the manager to motivate them. This may be in terms of a vision or a path.
8. Recognition – Employees may want to be recognized by their manager.

9. Resourcing – Employees may need the manager to provide resources.
10. Leverage – Employees may need the manager to act as leverage on others either within the team or partners.
11. Culture – The employee wants the manager to set the values and decision-making boundaries of the team.
12. Broader Status – The employee may need the manager to provide status on other projects outside their purview.
13. Pay/Benefits – The employee holds the manager accountable for setting appropriate pay and benefits for the employee.

Sample manager needs from employee:

1. Status – The manager may need explicit status of projects from employees.
2. Wisdom – The manager may need to go beyond the status and extract knowledge from the employee. The manager may need to dive deep into the details to extract wisdom.
3. Training – The manager may need the employee to train them.
4. Results – The manager needs the employee to deliver on goals.

One way to use the above list is to think through your 1:1 agendas. What needs are frequently re-occurring from you or your employee? Are there items that are outside of the above list? Do certain areas cause more tension in the relationship? By understanding what needs are coming up you can better tune your conversations to meet the needs of both you and your employee.

As a manager, you should reflect on the needs of the employee per topic. When the employee speaks (or emails) with you, take a minute to consider what the employee's spoken (or unspoken) need is. What is the language used by the employee? What is their demeanor? Is this topic a frequent discussion point or a new area? Before responding, take a minute to consider the needs of the employee, your needs, the relationship's needs, and the company's needs. By balancing and aligning these four needs you can provide a response that is beneficial to the long-term performance of all four entities.

FAQ
1. I'm friends with my employees. How does this change our relationship?
Friendship is a different type of relationship than an employee/manager relationship or a mentor/mentee relationship. Most often we have one relationship type with a person but occasionally we can have more than one. Work with your HR to understand policies or questions about managing friends. This can be especially important in romantic or familial relationships.

Ensure that both parties understand in each situation which relationship takes precedence. When you are having a performance review, the manager/employee relationship is paramount. When you are relaxing on vacation, the friendship comes first. Open communication with the employee and with your HR representative can ensure both relationships remain healthy.

2. I'm not getting along with an employee; what's wrong?
People are people. After defining the manager/employee relationship you may still not get along with your employee. Think through if that tension is putting extra strain on yourself, your employee, or your business. You may not always get along with your employees, but if it is not causing strain it may be fine to let it be. However, if you are in frequent tension and that tension is impacting yourself, your employee, or your business seek outside help. Speak with your HR representative, your manager, or your mentor. In worst cases, it may require an outside individual to come in and discuss the situation with each of you. Your responsibility as the manager is to act if you feel the tension is damaging.

3. My employee says that I am micro managing him/her. Or my employee says that I am too hands off. What should I do? The first is thing to understand your employee's needs. The second is to understand to explain your needs. It may be what they expect from you differs from what you thought they needed from you. Get into specifics, what behaviors or actions did you take in the past week that caused the employee to feel that way? If the expectations are set appropriately, determine if you both meeting those expectations. Often, we may say we want one thing but our actions show something else. Take a moment to do an honest assessment of your behavior. Speak with your manager, your mentor, or your peers. How do they see the situation? What would they do differently? Meet with your employee and identify a behavior that you would like to change. How can you hold each other accountable for identifying when that behavior occurs and how to change it?

4. My employee undermines me in front of others. What should I do? Speak to them about the situation. What is your business culture on challenging management? Companies vary on how much employees can argue/disagree with management. Work with your manager to

understand the culture and how it applies in various situations. Then speak to your employee. Offer them alternative ways of expressing their concern.

5. My employee doesn't provide me any feedback on how the relationship or my management tactics are working. What should I do?
It can be difficult for some individuals to speak to an authority figure about a relationship. There are deep personal and cultural norms outside of the company that may impact the willingness of an employee to discuss these issues. Speak with your HR representative. They may have alternative ways of capturing this information for you.

6. I want my employees to like me. I want my employees to respect me. I want my employees to fear me.
In all these cases look for the deeper need underlying this relationship dynamic. Why do you want employees to like you? Why do you want to feel respected? Is fear really what you want out of the relationship? It may take several rounds of discussion with HR, your mentor, or outside professionals to get to a deeper understanding of why you want that type of relationship. Look back at your own experiences growing up. How did you

engage with authority? Look at your school or your early professional career. How did you engage with management? Are there situations outside of the office that you are bringing to the employee/manager relationship? Are they overpowering your needs and the employee's needs within the relationship?

Questions to review after reading the chapter

1. How would you define the relationship with you manager? What are needs to do you have? Are they getting filled?
2. Think back on the manager you liked working with the most. What worked well within the relationship? What about your worst manager? What was difficult about working with them? What patterns emerge with these two extremes?
3. For each employee that you manage, write down what you believe his or her two primary needs are. Think through your last few interactions with them. Have your interactions helped fulfill those needs for your employees?

Questions to review after 3 months of 1:1s

1. Have you clearly defined your expectations of the employee/manager relationship with your employees? How did they respond?

2. Are the relationships you have with your
    employees better or worse?
3. How much time have you spent thinking
    about your employee/manager
    relationships? Have you discussed the
    relationships with your manager, mentor,
    or peers? Are there relationships that are
    operating more effectively than others?
4. What needs have you been successful at
    meeting with your employees? What needs
    have you failed to address?

7 - Effective Communication

As a manager, you will need to communicate with your employees in a unique way. This chapter provides you with several techniques to improve your communication. Strong interpersonal communication skills will make you a better manager and leader.

What is success?

Effective communication conveys information in a format where that the message is received and understood.

How do you do it?

This chapter is broken into several sections depending on the communication method you are using.

Communication Channels

To determine what communication channel to use, ask yourself what is the most effective way of conveying this information. In a work setting there are numerous communication pathways. Each pathway is unique in the speed of information, immediacy, and nuance provided.

1. **Instant Message/Slack** – This type of communicating channel is often used in professional environments. IM has an expectation of immediacy from the receiver. Due to the fact that the communication is written it can be slow to convey information. In addition, IMing lacks nuance. There is no facial or body

language conveyed. When I was a new manager, I often had to coach my team to GET UP from their chairs and walk over to the individual they were IMing when they were discussing complex situations.

2. **Email** – Email lacks the immediacy of IM (depending on your company), however it allows for additional data transmission, and has a degree of permanence. Like IMing, because the communication is written in can be slow to convey information. Each firm has a unique culture in the types and styles of emails that are appropriate. Some organizations encourage longer emails, while some send one sentence emails.

3. **1 to 1 phone calls** – Direct phone calls are often underutilized in corporate environment. A quick IM to verify the person is free followed up with a phone call can speed up information exchange. A phone call has less immediacy, as many people let phone calls go directly to voice mail. Being verbal, phone calls can convey more information than written forms, and has some degree of nuance based on tone of voice.

4. **1 to Many phone calls (conference calls)** – The conference call is the bane of many professional environments. The lack of visual cues and physical presence causes employees to speak over one another or cause employees to disengage. You aren't

accountable for your body language and may not be as deeply engaged as you would be in a 1 to 1 phone call. Conference calls can be effective if they are well managed. Consider the number of the attendees. Expecting a group of more than 4 people to contribute is unlikely to happen in a conference call. Another alternative to the conference call is the broadcast call. The differences are significant. A discussion conference call is one in which you want to have multiple parties contribute the call. You want discussion on a topic. A broadcast call is a one-way push of information; it is like giving a speech or presentation over the phone. Both conference calls and broadcast calls can become frustrating for all involved if the technology doesn't cooperate. Ensure that you understand the details of your conference call system. Calls tend to break or turn off completely at the most inopportune time. Have the back-up numbers memorized, request 2 conference IDs, one primary and one as a backup. Understand how to mute individuals, how to mute yourself, etc.

5. **1 to 1 Video Conference** – Similar to the conference call utilizing a 1 to 1 video conference can exchange more information. You can get facial expression along with the verbal communication. Video conference speeds are now at a level

where it feels natural to speak to each other. One persistent flaw is the location of the camera vs. the screen. Practice looking at the camera vs. the screen when speaking to someone. When looking at a screen you can appear to be looking over their shoulder, which can be disconcerting.

6. **1 to Many Video Conference** – Technology is improving for 1 to Many video conferences. At the time of this writing (2016) I have yet to see effective 1 to Many video conferences that are collaborative beyond 4 to 5 people. The technology has not made an 8 or 10 person video teleconference work successfully.

7. **1 to 1 Meetings** – As mentioned in the Effective 1:1 section, an in person 1:1 meeting can convey a great deal of information and nuance. You are using verbal communication along with body language. If you are discussing any topic where there could be an emotional response a 1:1 in person meeting is the most effective. This includes performance evaluations, managing out, etc. Consider the location of your 1:1. There are subtle dynamics at play based on the location of the meeting and where you are sitting. Meeting across a desk or table has a different feeling than meeting with nothing between you. Sitting at the ends of a table is different than sitting 90 degrees to each

other. A coffee shop 1:1 feels different than one held in your office. Determine what you want to covey and choose a location and seating arrangement appropriate to that. Don't fire an employee in a coffee shop, likewise, don't expect a collaborative discussion to occur if you are seated across a large desk from your employee

8. **1 to Many Meetings** – Just as with the 1 to many phone calls, for 1 to many meetings you should first identify if you are having a collaboration meeting or a broadcast meeting. These two types of meetings are different in their approach. A collaboration meeting will have a different agenda, expectations, etc.. The physical environment of a collaboration meeting is likely to be different than a broadcast. Collaboration may be better in a circle layout, and a broadcast will be more effective with the audience in rows (theatre-seating style).

Document Types

Managers often fail to consider the document format to use when communicating with others. Deciding to use a written document, PowerPoint, or interactive tutorial, etc. is an important step in conveying information. Don't just default to your personal preference; think about what the audience will expect and what will convey your information in the most accurate and efficient manner. I have worked in environments where everything was written in word and in environments where everything was PowerPoint. What matters most is your firm's culture. Understand the culture and reflect it back to your employees, peers, and manager through your documents.

Document Formats

With regards to the formats of documents, your employees will likely need your advice on what your company expects. Take a few minutes and state what your expectations are. What font do you use? What font size? Do you expect page numbers? Confidential footers? Stating your expectations will limit the churn your employees have when formatting their documents.

Language

Language is a powerful tool that is often overlooked by new managers. Companies have unique dialects. Each firm will have different ways of using language to convey meaning. As a manager, spend time reflecting on the specific words that you, your leadership, and your team use. Do leaders use "will do" or "could do"? Does the company use "we" or "you" when communicating? Understanding the nuances of your firm's dialect will allow you to communicate most effectively with your employees and your customers.

Agendas, Note Taking, and Action Items

Agenda, Note Taking, and Action Items are the most powerful tool you have to ensure the success of your business. These techniques are often underutilized. They take up time you have for other work, and often aren't valuable in the moment. But used properly they will make a dramatic change in your team.

Agendas – Agendas are a way of controlling the outcome of a meeting. To set an effective agenda consider the end state of the meeting. What do you want to have accomplished at the end of the meeting? Is it awareness of an idea? Feedback? A decision? An agenda is a map; it should lead you to your destination. Companies have various cultures related to the specific design of agenda. Ensure you understand your company's culture and that you can apply the agenda to accomplish your goal.

Notes – Notes are a way to capture the context of a meeting. Think of notes as preempting future questions. One of my earliest jobs was in was a consulting firm. We would often travel internationally to meet with clients. The firm would fly a dedicated note taker out to each meeting. After a full day of meetings and a dinner, we would gather back in the hotel and spend several hours refining the notes captured during the day. The next day, we would review the notes with the client and get formal approval of the notes. Initially, I was amazed at this investment of time in effort just for taking notes. We were all in the same meeting, what was the point of all this investment? However, the importance of effective notes became very clear to me the first time there was a disagreement about how a certain feature should work. We were able to look back at the notes and confirm exactly what was discussed. This saved the firm substantial amount of time and money rebuilding a feature. Proper notes address all decisions made or confirmed in the meeting. It can be less useful to capture all the lead up to the decision.

Action Items – Action items are the specific tasks that come out of a meeting. Write up all action items, assign owners to each and, and delivery dates from each meeting. Ensure you have a process to follow up on action items. This is the critical step that is often missed. Individuals walk out of the meeting with best intentions but then fail to ensure accountability with the action items. Use Excel, JIRA, or a similar tracking mechanisms to capture the action item. Be explicit to ensure compliance: when do you expect the items to be completed and by whom. Schedule a meeting to review the progress of the action items.

FAQ
    1. How can I keep up with my email?

There are various techniques you can learn to manage your incoming email. Here are some basic recommendations.

1. One Touch – Touch each email only once, 1) Delete, 2) File, 3) Respond (<5 min) 4) Create a task. (>5 Min) – By reducing the time you re-read an email you can speed up your processing.

2. Embrace Rules – Emails can be considered as a river. There are high flow and low flow times of day. Have rules that shuttle email into various folders and then review them when you have time. Some emails are interesting but not critical. Those you can move to a folder you rarely read if ever. There are some emails that are important but not urgent. Put those into a different folder.

3. Goals Based Folders – Create rules that send emails automatically into folders based on your goals. This can help reduce time spent searching for specific emails related to goals.

2. I am afraid of public speaking and Broadcast Meetings make me nervous. How can I improve my public speaking skills?
   I have seen great results with Toastmaster International. Often there will be a local group in your company or city. Make time to attend their classes and practice.

3. I feel like I'm talking past my employee. They aren't "getting it".
   This is a surprisingly common occurrence. Communication is a core skill of managers. New managers often have not been put in a position where they need to communicate with a wide variety of people. There will be a time when you will struggle to connect with an employee. One technique is to take time reviewing how the employee likes to take in information. Ask probing questions on how they best learn information. Do they like to read? Do they need to go back and think about a problem? Do they want to "talk it out"? One additional technique is the use of personality tests or training. DISC, Meyer's Briggs, Insights etc. are tools that can be used to understand how employees best receive, process, and exchange information. Utilize them to help better understand your team.

Questions to review after reading the chapter
   1. Review your calendar. Do you know the communication channel used in each meeting? Is it effective? Do you need to change the format of the meeting?
   2. Do you have standard templates you use for your documents? Does your team know where to find them?

3. What is your classification of documents? Do you have a structured storage plan? SharePoint? Wikis? Etc. When was the last time you couldn't find a document?
Think back to the last important meeting you led. Did you accomplish what you wanted your goal for the meeting? What changed in your business because of that meeting? What actions were taken because of that meeting?

8 - Effective 1:1s

One on Ones are an effective way of managing individuals. The 1:1 is a meeting dedicated to the manager/employee relationship; it is used to accomplish several management tasks between the manager and the employee. Effective 1:1s will improve your skills as a manager and the business results of your team.

What is success?

An effective 1:1 is a meeting in which the manager and employee walk away with their expectations met of the meeting. The manager and employee will often have different goals for the meeting. State those goals up front and ensure they are achieved.

When do you do it?

1:1s are typically held on a weekly or bi-weekly basis. Onboarding a new employee may require multiple 1:1s in each week. For employees that are more self-reliant a monthly 1:1 may be more appropriate. The length of the 1:1 differs depending on the employee and the situation. Don't be afraid to adjust the number and length of 1:1s based on the situation.

How do you do it?

There are some basics techniques that help ensure 1:1s are effective.

1. Agenda – An agenda is often overlook part of a 1:1. Since both the manager and the employee may have differing expectations

of the 1:1, it is important to construct a joint agenda. Having a clear agenda will ensure both parties get what they want out of the conversation.

2. Communication Styles – Remember that individuals have various communication styles. Apply your understanding of how best to communicate with an employee to your 1:1s. Some employees may need additional time to process topics or questions. While some perform the best with 100% verbal communication. Reflect on the ways that you and employee communicate best.

3. Topic Selection – There are a few standard buckets of topics that are reviewed in 1:1s.

   a. Project Status – A 1:1 may be used to provide status to the manager from the employee on current project status. Where is the team/employee performing against goals and what actions are being taken against goals? This is the most common topic area but it is important to not let project status be the only topic discussed in a 1:1

   b. Coaching and Development – A 1:1 should be used to coach and develop an employee. Reviewing a past situation or an upcoming situation provides an employee time to reflect on their performance. As a manager, you can use the opportunity to provide guidance to an employee. One tip is to designate a specific week of the month to development. The first 1:1 of the month can be the development 1:1 with time explicitly set apart to focus on professional development.

c. Performance Feedback – Using a 1:1 to provide semi-real time feedback on performance is critical to an effective annual review. Take the time to provide your thoughts on how the employee is performing against goals and values of the team. Keep performance feedback as a standing topic weekly or monthly to ensure that an annual review is not a surprise.

d. Partner/peer/manager feedback – A 1:1 is a great time to capture feedback on your team members' thoughts on your performance, your partner teams, or peer teams.

e. Problem Solving – An overlooked aspect of 1:1s is to use the time to collaboratively solve problems. By meeting with your employee as equals you can co-develop solutions to technical or business problems. Setting expectations with employees that problem solving is accepted and encouraged allows you to maintain a hand in the reality of the business.

FAQ
1. How often and for how long should 1:1s
   be?
   1:1s should be balanced against your
   other responsibilities, your needs, and the
   needs of your employees. What topics do
   you need to address in your 1:1s? How
   long should it take to address them? How
   much time does each employee use?
   Change the time and frequency of 1:1s
   based on each individual situation. Early in
   my career I set 1:1s to be the same
   amount of time and frequency for
   everyone. That ended up with some
   individuals not getting enough time and
   others getting too much time. Every 4-6
   weeks evaluate how your 1:1s are going
   with each employee. Do you need more
   time or more frequent 1:1s? Are you
   blocking progress against goals by not
   having enough 1:1s? Likewise, are they too
   frequent and getting in the way of
   progress? If the 1:1s are used to prioritize,
   set direction, etc. then you won't be a
   bottleneck to the business.

2. Are there other ways to have 1:1s?
   Yes! Some employees (or managers) may
   prefer to hold 1:1s in alternative fashion.
   As you go from an in person 1:1, to email
   (for example), the amount of time you will
   need for the 1:1 increases. A 1:1 conveys a
   great deal of subtle information. You need

to ensure you are getting (and broadcasting) those nuances in whatever format you use. For several years in my career I reported to managers that were remote. I always spent more time with them when 1:1s were on the phone vs. when I had a chance to meet with them in person. We could convey more information quickly when we met in person.

3. The team is meeting their goals; do I still need to meet with them? I hold scrums/team meetings, why do I need to meet with my employees individually? 1:1s exist beyond status reports. Review the above list of topics. If you can discuss each topic fully with your employees outside of 1:1s on a consistent basis please let me know and I'll update this question with your technique.

4. My employees talk about different topics in their 1:1s. Is this normal? Yes, employees are not robots. They have different passions, emotions, and careers. You can have the same two people working on the same project in the same role and level and have vastly different 1:1s. Embrace the diversity; respond to the individual needs and treat each 1:1 as a unique opportunity to impact your team.

Questions to review after reading the chapter
1. Do you have 1:1s with your Manager? How long/frequent are they?
2. Review the list of topics in your 1:1s with your manager over the past few weeks? Are there patterns of topics? Are you addressing all the areas that you want to discuss? What things can you stop discussing? What should you start discussing?
3. Setup your 1:1s with your employees now. Start with 30 minutes every week if necessary. Talk to your peer managers and ask how often do they meet with their employees.

Questions to review after three months of 1:1s
1. What have you learned about your employees?
2. Are you spending the right amount of time with each employee? Are there 1:1s that you are struggling to fill? Are there 1:1s that you always run out of time?
3. Are you deliberate with the use of time? Do you always have an agenda?
4. Are there specific topics you haven't addressed with your employee? Are you finding it hard to talk about career paths, for example? How can you carve out time to ensure you are addressing that topic?

9 - Time Management

Effective time management is the key to success for all employees, and it is essential for a manager. A manager has greater flexibility and responsibility in how they use their time than his or her employees. As a manager, you must set up systems to track and monitor where your time is spent so you can be deliberate about how you allocate your time. Where you spend, your time will determine your professional success.

What is Success?

Managers who are deliberate about time management have clear goals regarding how they want to spend their time and they often utilize systems to track their time allocation. Successful time management means spending the right amount of time on the right priorities. Unsuccessful managers let external forces determine their time; successful managers drive compliance of their own time.

When do you do it?

Successful time management requires periodic review of how you spend your time. A weekly or monthly analysis of where you want your time to be spent vs. where it was spent is a valuable task.

How do you do it?

Managers fail when they don't create space to manage their time. To be successful you must prioritize the act of time management. Below are three steps to effective time management.

1. **Forecast Your Time** - The first step towards successful time management is the setting and prioritization of goals. Where would you like to spend your time? Where would you be best able to improve your team or your business? Once you have a mental picture of where you would like to spend your time, begin bucketing your time into various categories. Don't get carried away; you are likely only working 40-60 hours a week. Having more than 10 categories will not add any additional value in managing your time. Keep it simple and add categories later if necessary.

Some potential categories to utilize:

- Legal & Policy - What are legal or policy based time blocks? Do you need to review expense reports? Do you need to attend HR briefing on security? Etc.
- Broadcasting Information – These time blocks are designated for communicating out information to various teams. This encompasses all status updates via email or business reviews. Be sure to include the time you spend preparing this information for consumption.

- Receiving Information – These are time blocks where you are reading or taking in information. This often includes email or business reviews.
- Email - Often email is setup as a separate category as it can consume a great deal of your time as a manager.
- 1:1s – One on Ones should be tracked as a separate category as they are unique meetings in which you are explicitly managing individuals.
- Goal Based Allocation – Each critical goal can be tracked as a separate bucket of time. Should you be spending more or less time on your goals? Are you allocating your time on the most critical goals for your business?
- Travel – If you spend a significant amount of time in travel, make sure you add it as an explicit category.

Once you have your time categories defined, set the number of hours you would like to spend on each category per week. Do not look at your calendar at this stage. Envision a blank slate: Where do you think it is most critical for you to spend time? After you allocate those hours build a simple chart that lists each category as a percentage of a week.

2. **Track Your Time** - Once you have a target in mind for how you want to spend your time, begin tracking your calendar. There are various ways to do this. (Outlook is great at this.) At a high level, you want every hour of your day assigned to one category. Do not double tag categories. Double tagging will lead to double counting your hours. Don't have empty slots in your calendar. Keep it simple. If you spend 3 hours equally on 3 different tasks, it does not matter exactly when you were working on each task. Simply create three items and block each for an hour. At the end of the week all your working hours should be covered with a meeting or item. Each meeting/item should be tagged with one category, preferably by color; this process allows you to quickly identify the major buckets of time spent. Sum up all your categorized hours and the number of hours you spent per category. This will give you a percentage of time in each category.

3. **Analyze Your Time** - Upon looking back at your week, you have a target percentage of time and an actual percentage of time. Do they match? If so, great job; keep it up! If not, spend some time thinking about why the percentages don't match? Were your forecasts incorrect? Do you feel your actual time

spent is better for the business than your forecasts?

Before making any significant adjustments to your time I recommend performing the three steps listed above (forecast, track, analyze) for several weeks. Often managers time allocation fluctuate week over week as business rhythms change. After a month, you will likely begin to see patterns. You may need to adjust your categories. For example, you may notice that the first week of the month is more or less busy than the middle of the month.

Once you have forecast, tracked, and analyzed for several weeks it is time to take control of your calendar. Start by looking at the next week. Categorize all items on your calendar. Based on that categorization, what needs to change? To change your time allocation, you have two actions to take 1) Stop doing something or 2) Start doing something.

To stop doing something means to not attend a meeting or not spend time on certain tasks. Analyze those tasks you feel are not matching your time allocation forecasts. What would happen to the business or your team if you stop attending a particular meeting or stopped doing a specific task? Are there other individuals (team members or partners) that would be better suited to accomplish the task? Can you perform the tasks differently and still get value out of it? Can you cut the time by 80% but still get 80% of the value of the task? Don't shoot for perfection, instead try to eliminate or modify 1 to 2 items in the first week.

Now that you plan on stopping something, ask yourself where you should spend more time. Where are there holes in your calendar that you can be deliberate in filling? If you remove items, can you fill that space with more impactful work? Don't shoot for the moon but begin by adding in 1 or 2 items in the first week.

After the first week of adjustment continue to forecast, track, and analyze your time each week. It may take several months to align your time to your forecasts. Once your time spent is aligned to your forecast, it is likely you can shift to a monthly-based view of your time. Do not ever stop this analysis. Effective allocation of your time as manager is critical for your success. Spending an hour each month to ensure that you are working on the right things is critical to your success.

FAQ

1. I don't understand this categorization nonsense! Help!
   If the process is too complicated, just take a piece of paper and write down 1 line per every half hour. Next, write down the category for each half hour block. After that add up all the half hour blocks per

category, divide that number by 2 and that is how many hours you spent on that category.

2. My customers determine how I spend my time; I don't control my calendar.
   Even in a sales management job, you have a responsibility to effectively utilize your time for the benefit of your company. Are you meeting with the right customers? Are you spending the right time with customers vs. your team? Was a meeting the best use of your time?

3. My manager determines how I spend my time; I don't control my calendar.
   Speak with your manager about where your time is going. Having your time managed by others is disempowering. As you are now a manager, you have been identified as someone who can take on more responsibility. What is preventing your manager from given you the responsibility of your time? Are there steps you can take to demonstrate to your manager that they can trust you to manage your time?

4. My assistant manages my calendar; how does this change the technique?
   The only change here is to complete your forecast, track, and analyze step with your assistant. They should understand where

you want to spend your time and should help rearrange your time allocation as much as possible to meet your ideal state. It is helpful, in this situation, to rank the activities that you are asked to do every day. Be clear with them on what takes priority in your schedule.

5. I have too much to do; I can't fit it all in. Or I'm working xxx number of hours; I'm burning out.
   When you find yourself in this situation there are few techniques to consider.
   a) Is this temporary? Often businesses go in cycle with high and low cycles. Are you in a high cycle? When it will end?
   b) Who is applying these expectations of your time? Does the firm have a culture of working xxx hours? If so, that may be very difficult to change. Perhaps your manager has put a long list of deliverables on your plate. Speak with them about which items can be moved to others, postponed, or simply not performed. Are you putting these expectations on yourself? Managers are often high performers and may expect too much of themselves. Be strict about stopping tasks. What would happen if x didn't happen? Would you go to jail? Would you get fired? After those two questions, there is a huge amount of

ambiguity on the importance of a task.
Be brutal in killing tasks.

c) Work is like insulation. It grows to fill
the space given it. You need to ensure
you are constraining that work. Set
boundaries for yourself. What would be
an appropriate amount of time spent
working? Are there certain hours that
you can move work into? The advent of
technologies that allow us to work from
any location offers risks and benefits.
Make sure the technology is working
for you.

Questions to review after reading the chapter

1. Without looking, where do you believe you
spend your time?
2. What task did you do this week that you
can stop doing?
3. What didn't you get done this week that
you can add to your calendar?
4. How do your manager, your peers, and
your mentor manage their time? Are there
techniques they use that you can try?

Questions to review after forecasting, tracking, and allocating your time for three months

1. Did you present this idea to your
employees? This technique can work for
anyone who has some degree of autonomy
over his or her time.

2. How close are you to your ideal allocation? 50%? 90%? What's preventing you from meeting that ideal? The last few meetings and tasks will be the most difficult to remove. You cut the easy stuff already.
3. Can you tell how many hours you spent on each goal? Did you spend more or less time on goals that were successful?
4. Try this technique on your time outside of work. Are you spending your personal time the way you want to?

10 - Constraints Based Innovation

As a manager, you will need to drive innovation for your team. There are many techniques to foster innovation in a professional environment. Constraints Based Innovation is a technique I have used successfully for innovation within my business. This concept was first presented to me by Professor David Owens when I was attending Vanderbilt University. Ten years later, I am still utilizing it.

Constraints Based Innovation is a technique used to identify what constraints or limits exist on a given problem or business and what the problem or business looks like if those constraints they are removed.

What is Success?

Success with Constraints Based Innovation is measured when, after applying the technique, you understand what your constraints are and what would occur if they were removed (or added).

How to practice Constraints Based Innovation?

Constraints Based Innovation can be thought of as a series of circles enveloping a given point.

Select a problem space. Here, as an example, we will use revenue. Draw a dot on a piece of paper. That represents your current revenue. Now put a dot in the upper right (always good when revenue goes up and to the right). That's your end state; you want increased revenue.

Now consider the factors that are preventing you from achieving increased revenue. For example, customers may be getting in the way. Next, draw a circle around your starting point to represent your customers. Perhaps another inhibition is production; draw another circle to represent production.

Here's the critical part: when you draw the second circle if you draw a line between your starting revenue and your ending revenue, which circle is intersected first? For instance, 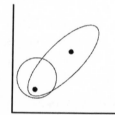 if customers are currently limiting you, then that circle would be smaller than the production. If on the other hand, production is limiting you, then the production circle would be smaller than customers. Now add 2 or 3 more circles: pricing, competitors, etc. How do all those intersect? Which of those is the FIRST constraint? Which is the SECOND constraint? What constraint isn't preventing you from hitting your revenue?

By identifying these constraints, you can begin to prioritize what needs to change so you can move from where you are to your end state.

The model can also be used in reverse. Let's say that you draw a second dot down and to the left of your end state to represent what would happen if constraints became tighter. What would happen if a new competitor entered the market? What would happen if one of your factories closed? By identifying what occurs when new constraints are added into your business, you can determine where your business is most at risk.

A similar technique can be used for prioritization of your team's work. Take your current resources and cut them in half. What tasks would you focus on to sustain your business? What if you doubled your resources? What would you focus on in that case? Thinking of your business as a series of constraints and how those constraints interact can be a useful technique to innovate.

FAQ

1. How does constraints based innovation differ from "thinking outside the box"?
   Thinking outside the box model puts the onus on the individual to identify an arbitrary end state. The box is the existing sets of constraints. The constraints based model breaks down the box into tangible constructs.

2. What's the drawback of constraints based innovation?
   One of the drawbacks is that it orients the user to the existing business reality. It anchors the mind to consider what is

happening today. It can be difficult to make extreme leaps in innovation while using constraints based innovation. For example, creating an entirely new industry may be difficult using constraints based thinking. However, constraints based innovation is extremely useful for determining what is holding back your team or a given product.

3. How can I apply constraints based innovation in a team setting?
I have used constraints based model to open discussions about how individuals view a given business. I first take a few minutes to describe the technique, then I ask everyone on my team to build their own set of circles. Next, I ask them to share their ideas with the group. Typically, several constraints will be the same, but often my team identifies new constraints that I hadn't considered.

Questions to Review after reading the chapter
1. What constraints can you quickly identify that are limiting your business? What are you doing to remove those constraints?
2. What would happen if you doubled your employees? What if you had to give up half of them?

3. What is the one metric that defines your team? Would you choose revenue, cost, or profit?
4. When will you block out 30 minutes on your calendar to practice this technique?

Questions to review after practicing the constraints based innovation technique

1. What was the most difficult aspect of the technique?
2. What new insights did you gather by utilizing the technique?
3. What actions will you take now that you have this information? Will you request more/different resources? Will you set new goals? The technique is only valuable if you act against what you learned.
4. How will you teach this to your team? What will you learn from them? Are you prepared to change the direction of your team based on what you learn?

11 - Status Reporting

Part of your responsibility as a manager is to report on the status and health of the business. Status reporting varies by team. Regardless of those variants, there are two buckets of updates that should always be addressed: project status and business metrics. Whether you report on projects or metrics or both, it is important to have a set rhythm to publish your team's impact.

What is Success?

Reporting on status is primarily for the benefit of other groups and your management chain. A successful status reporting plan ensures that the right people know the right information at the right time.

There is additional benefit to status reporting for you and your team. Goals are one of the two areas on which employees are evaluated. By having an ongoing status report process you can quickly address areas of gaps with an employee. Without a clear status reporting process, you may end up not addressing gaps in performance until it is too late to correct.

When do you do it?

As the goal of status reporting is to provide the right information to the right people at the right time, when you send status reporting varies depending on the information and the people consuming it. Below are examples of various types of status reports:

1. Daily Status Report - A daily status report is appropriate for critical projects that require multi-stakeholders to move forward together. Typically written by the project owner, a daily flash report is a report of raw data. It is a snapshot of business metrics that are important for the health of a business.

2. Weekly Status Report - A weekly project status report that provides Red/Yellow/Green (R/Y/G) goal update is an easy way for you and your partners to quickly assess what projects are at risk. It also provides a good forum for team members to escalate issues or request help.

3. Weekly Business Metric Review - Weekly business metric review meetings allow you to quickly jump on issues while not overwhelming the business by spending all your time generating business metrics.

4. Monthly Status Report - A monthly project status report should offer deeper commentary than just R/Y/G. This report is a good way to provide a more detailed discussion of the patterns that are evolving across projects. Is there a specific team member or partner group that is blocking multiple projects? Is there a gap in skills on the team? Is there a need for more or less resourcing? Your monthly project status report should discuss these questions.

5. Monthly Business Metric Review - Monthly business metrics reviews allow you to tease out long-term patterns within your business. By looking at multiple weeks of data you can begin to identify patterns.

6. Quarterly Status Report - Quarterly status reporting is appropriate for businesses that are stable and operating efficiently. The quarterly status report allows only four times during the year to review data and adjust. Quarterly reporting should, therefore offer deep insights on the business and broadcast significant shifts in prioritization and investments.

How do you do it?
Status reporting should be thought of a seesaw. On one end is the cost of providing status reporting; on the other end is the need for you, your partners, and your management to understand the state of your business. As a manager, it is your job to minimize the cost of creating status reports while providing appropriate depth to your stakeholders.

A mental model to use is a one-touch status reporting process. A one-touch status process means that any project update is only touched once in the process. Many hours can be wasted by each chain in a status reporting process editing lower employee's updates. This should be eliminated. A manager should not have to edit a status provided by a team member. To perform a one-touch status process everyone on the team must fully understand the requirements for completing a status report.

Project Status Updates
A simple way to manage project status updates
is to have a master spreadsheet of goals. The
rows should list the goals on your team and the
columns should list the goal description, the
owner, goal date, R/Y/G, status, and requests for
help. By having a master sheet for your team,
individual owners can write weekly updates as to
the state of their project. As the manager, you
will have a quick visual view of the health of your
projects. Ideally this status report can be re-used
for monthly and quarterly status updates. An
alternative management tool would be to update
the R/Y/G and request help on a weekly basis.
From there, you update your grid with additional
written commentary monthly.

Goal Description	Owner	Goal Date	R/Y/G	Status	Request for Help
Release Book	Sean	8/1/2017	G	Finalizing last draft	
Launch Website	Kristin	7/1/2017	Y	Risk due to competing priorities	Need additional reviewers
Create Training	Pam	10/1/2017	G	Initial draft complete	

Business Metrics Updates
Business metrics reports are more complex than
project status updates because decisions on
business metrics are often more difficult to make
than project decisions. For projects, you are
often applying new or different resources or
making decisions whether to go with option A or
option B. For business metrics, it can be difficult
to determine what to measure, or even how to
decide what action to take about the metric.

When thinking about business metrics consider
the fact that the purpose of providing business
metric updates is to decide what action to take.

To identify your metrics, you need to understand what potential decisions or actions can be taken in your business. What levers are you able to move to guide the direction of your business? What can you move in terms of resources? Where can you invest or de-invest? Once you understand your levers you need to identify what information you need to have to decide whether to make that investment/disinvestment. For example, revenue is a common business metric. If your revenue falls what will you do? Is measuring revenue by itself enough for you to decide where to invest? Probably not. You need additional information about why your product is missing its revenue target. You need to know which sales channel is struggling. Often you need 3-5 metrics to be able to take an action.

Input vs. Output Business metrics
An input metric is a measurement of an activity that is upstream of your business or team. An output metric is a measurement of what comes out of your team or business. It is important to monitor both types of metrics. The input vs. output metrics provides a good framework to understand how to speed up course corrections in your business. If you are managing a factory and your supplier stops providing parts, you need to act right when that halt occurs, not 3 weeks later when your sales fall because you haven't been producing any widgets. Make sure you're a measuring upstream and downstream metrics.

Documenting Business metrics
Before you begin reporting on business metrics, you must document each metric.

1. Description of the metric
2. How the metric is calculated
3. Forecast or +/- acceptable range
4. What actions to take if the metric falls out of the acceptable range

Often managers fail to document their business metrics. Then when the metric veers off course, they spend too much time trying to understand what action to take. Don't create a metric unless you can answer all the above points.

Publishing Business metrics
Only after you have identified and documented your business metrics should you publish them. Set up daily flash reports for the critical metrics for your team. Review these reports daily to identify any red flags. More in-depth weekly business metrics should be reviewed to identify what issues may be arising. Upon review, delegate action items and follow up on them regularly to drive changes based on the business metrics. Monthly metric reviews will identify long-term patterns and trends in the business metric. Again, action items will arise out of these reviews and those items should be tracked on a weekly basis.

FAQ

1. I have a lot of scorecards, but I can't figure out why my business is still failing. What do I do?

   There are two solutions. The first is that you have the right metrics but are making the wrong decisions. This is unlikely to be true. You were selected to be a manager and part of that is based on your business judgment and knowledge. Just to be sure, ask others what decisions they would make given the same set of metrics. The second and more likely reason is that you are measuring the wrong metrics. Often, metrics are tracked because "that's how it's always been done" or subtler "because that's what the tools allow us to track." Throw those excuses out the window. Get in a room with a big white board and begin describing your business. This may take 2 or 3 rounds to get a clear understanding. Effective metrics can make or break a business. Spend the time and human capital to measure the right things and you are more likely to succeed.

2. I want to monitor my customer's satisfaction with my business. How can I track that?

   There is a whole industry set up for measuring customer satisfaction. One simple model is net promoter score or net promoter indicator (NPI). Ask the following question: "How likely are you to recommend our business?" On a ten-point scale count the top 2 (9, 10s) and subtract the bottom 5 counts (5, 4, 3, 2, 1). That's your NPI score. Measure that on a periodic basis to see your trends. Do you notice the flaw in your metric? What action can you take from it? If your NPI goes up by a point what do you do? If it goes down, what to do you? NPI can be a simple barometer, but you must include explanatory metrics to be able to take a decision. In this case, the raw score is less valuable than the changes to that score over time.

3. Should I monitor my team's satisfaction? Or team health?
   This is an interesting question. I have seen this concept be successful and have seen it fail miserably. For teams that sit next to each other, and engage with each other frequently throughout the day, they will likely intuitively know their health score. For teams that are remote, or work in silos, a team satisfaction score may be appropriate. Be ready to respond to that score. What will you, as a manger, do if the score rises or falls? Do your expectations of what a successful score is match your team's expectations?

4. My team keeps providing me updates after I need them, so I have to bug them off-cycle. How can I get faster updates?
This often occurs when not enough time has been put into setting up a calendar of updates. Status updates should flow like a stream in the workplace. Front line updates -> manager updates -> group manager updates. Work towards the one touch model. This means you need to coordinate when your team will provide you with updates, so you can provide your manager with updates. Take a calendar and identify when you need to give updates, count back 1 or 2 days and make that the deadline for your team to provide updates. Put a reminder on everyone's calendar.

Questions to review after reading the chapter
1. Do you have a status report? How often is it reviewed?
2. How long does it take to update your status report?
3. Who is the consumer of your status report?
4. How often is a status provided via the status report and how often by other channels (emails, hallway, etc.)?

Questions to review after 6 months of status reporting
1. What improvements have you made to your status reporting?

2. Have you minimized status churn on your team?
3. If you haven't already, begin to track how many hours it takes you and your team to provide status reports. What can you do to reduce that time?
4. Are you utilizing the one touch method? If not, who is updating statuses more than once? Are you consolidating or editing information? What guidance can you give your team to reduce duplication of work?

12 - Career Paths

As a manager, you are partially responsible for coaching your team members on their individual careers. As a manager, you should think of yourself as a mentor or coach, rather than the owner of your employee's careers. A career belongs to the person. An individual's career involves hundreds of choices. As a manager, you are only privy to a small number of those choices. Coach and mentor, but do not dictate your employee's careers.

Good distinct

What is Success?

A successful career discussion with an employee is one in which it becomes clear what the expectations are for the employee to progress to his or her next role (either promotion or lateral). Notice success is <u>not</u> an explicit plan, a timeline, or a commitment. The world is full of ambiguity; your employee will want guarantees and timeframes. As a manger, you will be unable to provide that level of commitment. You can, however, provide as much clarity as possible on the expectations for the new role.

When do you do it?

It is important to keep an open and ongoing discussion with your employees regarding career path. Don't wait until an annual review. Maintain monthly or quarterly time meetings to discuss progress towards the next opportunity. During certain times, there may be a need to have more consistent discussions. Listen to your employee's needs and adjust as necessary, and never go more than a few months without a conversation.

How do you do it?
Approach a career path discussion with the following stages:

1. **Passion** – The identification of an individual's passion is often the most difficult component of the career discussion. People can find it difficult to identify what aspect of their current or former position excites them. One technique I use is the "home conversation". I ask an employee the following question: when you go home in the evening, what do you choose to discuss with your spouse, friend, or family? Often the employee will only have a few minutes to discuss their day. This constraint subconsciously forces the employee to identify what really matters to them about the day. What aspects of their job do they experience a lot of emotion around? Often these are areas the employee feels the most passion towards, either positive or negative. Asking them to document the topics they choose to discuss at home can help them identify their passion.

   Another helpful technique for determining an employee's passion is the "great day" model. I ask my employees to intentionally think about and document what days they feel the most joy. What days do they consider great? After they have had a few of those days, work with the employee to target what aspect of those days made it great. Why did they feel buoyant when they went home? What experiences in those particular days led them to feel that way?

2. **Skills** – Once the employee's passion is identified you should coach her or her to identify their skillset. Notice that skills and passion are not necessarily the same. I have skills that I am very good at, but I don't have passion for. Likewise, there are skills that I lack, but have strong passion for. There are various techniques to identify skills, but one way is to look at your company values or job descriptions. How you evaluate employees is often based on skills. Look at what skills the employee holds to identify gaps against their next possible position.

3. **Options** – Once an employee's passion and skills are identified, begin considering various roles for them. This is a good time to send the employee out to meet with numerous partners or other teams. Even if the team is not actively hiring, exposing the employee to new divisions or roles is an important component of exploring

options. Once the employee has identified two or three potential roles, sit down with them to discuss what attracts them to those new positions. What is the overlap between their current role and the new one? By identifying patterns, you can help expand the employee's options into various other positions. At this point it is important to not narrow down the search. If the employee becomes singularly focused on a specific role they may limit themselves if the position is filled or no longer needed. It is important to keep options open. Ask them to look at multiple positions that require the skills they are passionate about.

It is also important to teach the employee that there is rarely a perfect position. Walking a career path successfully is all about making the best choice at each point in time. I coach employees to find a role with at least 50% alignment. If you can feel yourself being passionate about at least 50% of the role than it is worth it to pursue. If the employee is passionate about less than 50% of the position, they will not thrive in the role.

4. **Gaps** - Once potential roles are identified, sit down with the employee and identify what gaps exist between their current set of skills and experiences and those that

the new roles require. Sometimes there will be few gaps, as the role may need little or no additional experiences. However, there can be times where there will be significant gaps between where the employee is and what their dream role requires. Be realistic, but positive in this conversation. Be specific in setting the bar. If you were interviewing for the new role, what type of questions would you ask? What responses would you expect to hear? This can help the employee understand where the bar is set.

Once the employee understands the bar, allow them to take the lead in identifying what experiences they can take on that would meet and fill those gaps. Are there specific trainings required? Are there projects they should take on? This is a scenario where your ability to see a wider scope than your employee can be helpful. Use your discretion to carve out unique opportunities to grow your employee. Are there existing projects that can be shifted? Are there special projects they can take on?

After your employee has begun to work on securing skills not previously in their repertoire, it is important to set a specific goal to track their progress. For example, if an employee is developing excel skills, you may ask them to build a financial model using excel by the end of the quarter. By setting an explicit goal for a career path, it signals to the employee that you expect them to work on the goal. The goal should be focused on the experiences and gaps of the employee. You would not hire someone just because they read a book or took a class. You want the employee to demonstrate a skill to the extent that you would hire them if they were an external candidate. Craft a goal to focus the employee as if you were going to interview them for the skill.

5. **Follow up** - After the goal is set, you should review it just as you would any other goal. While the employee won't be evaluated on their career progress, it is essential to keep tabs on their improvement. Doing so demonstrates your willingness to invest in the employee and it allows your employee to focus on their development. There are hundreds of professional and personal expectations set on an employee. Providing a regular opportunity for them to focus on their growth is an easy technique that builds rapport and trust between you and your employees.

FAQ

1. I want my employee to stay in their current role. Why would I help them find a new job?

   This is a frequent concern of new managers. It is difficult if an employee leaves your team. You may be asked to pick up the slack for that employee. Consider the impact of having the employee stay on the team. What is the long-term impact to the others on the team? They will know that the employee wants a different role and that you have blocked them. New employees will perceive themselves as trapped in their role. They may begin looking externally.

   Now consider the opposite. As a manager, you actively invest in developing your employees. You identify new opportunities for them to develop. You encourage them to explore new opportunities. They feel that you are invested in their success. They may leave but they will tell their friends, associates, and network that you helped them get their new role. They will pass along leads and referrals. Who knows? In a few years, they may want to come back.

2. My employee wants to change to an entirely different position.

Think of every new role as a risk management task. When looking at a new role, an employee should consider the amount of change they will experience by shifting to a new role. Employees certainly can be successful in entirely new roles, but the amount of change they will experience will be more significant than if they shifted to a parallel role. Here are the buckets of change to consider when shifting roles:

1. New Manager – Will the employee have a new manager?
2. New Partners – Does the employee must build new relationships?
3. New Goals – How aligned to the current goals are the goals in the new role?
4. New Industry – Is the role in the same industry or something entirely differently?
5. New Technology – Will the employee be using the same technology or new systems?

You and your employee should evaluate each bucket of change to see how many changes they will experience and the magnitude of those changes.

3. My employee has passion for a role, but I don't think they will be successful in that role.
As a manager, you are responsible for coaching and mentoring your employee. It

is not your role to prevent them from making a mistake. The employee owns their career. You can offer advice, or ask probing questions to understand what is attracting them to that position. You can help the employee identify the skills that they will need for the role. But ultimately it is the employee's choice to take on a new role.

Questions to review after reading the chapter
1. Think back on your career path. Was it a straight line from where you started to where you are today? A zig zag?
2. What are your passions? What do you go home and talk about?
3. What's the next stage of your career? Have you talked to your manager about that next step?

Questions to review after having a career discussion with all your employees
1. Do you know two potential roles for each employee?
2. Can you name the two most significant gaps for each employee?
3. Does each employee feel empowered to own their own career?
4. Have you made a commitment to each employee to review their process every few months?

13 - Performance Calibration

As a manager, you will be responsible for calibrating the members of your team against each other and against other teams. While there are various methodologies and processes to do this comparison, here we focus on your responsibilities as a manager within the calibration process. I have also included a section on promotions in this chapter, as promotions are often performed with and are similar in nature to calibrations. It's important to note the steps involved. In my model, employees are calibrated against their role. After you understand how the employee performs relatively to their role, you will then hold the actual performance evaluation. It is foolish to evaluate something if you don't have something to measure it against.

What is a successful calibration?

A successful calibration is one in which each employee is calibrated against an ideal employee for their role and level. For example you may multiple software engineers. A software engineer 1 who is right out of college is calibrated to a different bar than a software engineer 4 with 20 years of experience. Each employee should have a role and a level within that role. All managers must understand the ideal employee bar, so that the real employee's gaps (over or under the ideal) are consistently identifiable.

When do you calibrate?
Calibrations often occur on an annual or semi-annual basis and as close to the performance time window as possible.

How does calibration work?
There are several steps of the calibration process. These steps (listed below) are required for calibration, regardless of the specific details of your company's methodology.

Role & Level Understanding
The first step in calibration is to ensure that you understand the role and level against which you will be calibrating each employee. Often companies will have formal documents that lay out expectations of each role and level combination. Ask your HR partner for any such documentation to support you in this process. In addition, if you are managing a new role or a new level, ask your peers or mentors to provide you with their expectations. Often there are unstated guidelines or rules of thumb that companies use to evaluate employees.

One of my most difficult calibration meetings occurred when the managers involved had inconsistent understandings of a role. The managers (and HR) had failed to formally define the role and the levels within the role. Therefore, each manager came to the meeting with their own biases and assumptions. It took several hours for us to realize the problem was not with our teams, but with the lack of consistency in our expectation of what the role should accomplish. Since that experience, I always spend several weeks building a formal job description with expectations of each role and level. My calibration meetings always run much smoother as everyone has read and agreed to these expectations.

Documentation
After you understand the role and level for each employee, begin documenting each employee on two dimensions: first, the employee's performance against his or her goals and second, the employee's performance against the company's values. Evaluate each employee on the goals they accomplished and how they accomplished them. It is best to use a simple spreadsheet with each employee, his or her goals, and what company values they excels and the company values they needs to develop. Strive to present as accurately as possible the individual's performance over the evaluation time period. New managers tend to paint an overly positive portrait of their employees. Doing so is unfair to your employee, your company, and your peers. You must be honest to all parties involved. Your goal is to not <u>win</u> the calibration; your goal is to present an <u>accurate picture of reality</u>.

To help you prepare the documentation, review the specifics of each employee's goals. What were the salient points? What did the employee have to overcome? Was there anything exceptional or different about their performance against the goal? Use feedback from peers and partners. Pay attention to feedback on the company values the employee utilized to accomplish his or her goals. It is often easy to calibrate an employee's performance when measured against goals (Did x get launched by y date? Did they bring in z revenue?). But how the employee accomplishes that goal tends to be difficult to capture. As a manager, you may not be in the meetings or conversations where these company values are applied. Rely on your peers to help assess.

Discussion
At most companies, there will be a meeting to discuss employees across teams. You should come prepared with the above documentation. In addition to the document, you should prepare a short and a long narrative of your employee. Often managers will only have 1-2 minutes to describe each individual's performance. If that narrative aligns with your peers' expectations and paints a clear picture of the employee's performance, you may not be asked to elaborate. However, if there are questions, be prepared to speak 5-10 minutes in depth about an individual employee.

The calibration discussion can be a tense meeting for new managers. Large amounts of information are being shared, and many important decisions on promotions or pay are being decided. Come to the meeting prepared so you are not overwhelmed in the moment. Practice the narratives on each employee out loud ahead of time. Additionally, you will want to be sure that you are paying attention to not only what is said, but also the body language of those with whom you are meeting. Are your peers nodding or shaking their heads? Are there specific phrases that are used that everyone responds to positively or negatively? Calibration discussions often occur only once or twice a year, so come prepared and be engaged in these meetings.

Actions
After the discussion with the other managers, update your documentation to reflect any new information received at the meeting. Did your picture of the ideal employee change? Did you get new feedback from your peers? Managers often don't take the opportunity to update their own view of their employees with the new information that arises in the meeting. It is normal to feel hesitant about changing your point of view. Resist this feeling. Be open with your decisions and don't be afraid to refine your calibrations.

At this point you will transition into performance review process. Take the above information as you begin the process of writing reviews.

Promotions
A promotion can be thought of as an in-depth calibration of an employee against a higher-level

ideal employee. The process of determining a promotion is remarkably like that of calibration. Rather than evaluating the employee against the ideal employee at the current level, evaluate him or her against the ideal employee at the next level. What experiences would that ideal employee have? What goals would they have to accomplish? How do they utilize company values to accomplish tasks?

Once you have this picture, begin crafting a document to measure your employee against that new bar. A promotion is a significant event, and as such requires robust documentation and feedback for making your case. As with the calibration review, be sure you are highlighting gaps in their performance against this higher level. The point of a promotion meeting is not to sell the promotion, but to provide a clear picture of the next level and how this individual meets, beats, or misses it.

A mental model I use for both promotions and calibration is to think of a stereo equalizer. An equalizer is a device with a series of levers. The levers operate the volume of sound at a certain frequency. The levers have scales from +10 to 0 to -10. As you adjust the lever you can dial up or dial down that frequency. For this mental model, each frequency represents a goal or a company value. Consider the ideal employee being a 0 across all frequencies. This is the bar an employee must meet for their given level. How would you set the dials to represent the employee? In each area they out performing, move that lever to +5. In each area they are underperforming, move that lever to -5. Most employees will end up with a mix of positive and negatives.

FAQ

1. How do I calibrate someone who has just been promoted? Or will be promoted during the calibration?
A calibration is a review of past performance. You should calibrate the individual based on what level they had most recently (before the calibration). Another way would be to consider what level they were at for the longest time during the review period.

2. How do I calibrate someone who has been on leave?
You should contact your HR representative to understand your local laws and company policies regarding leave.

3. How do I calibrate someone who I have only managed for a short while?
You should meet with their prior manager and discuss their goals and how they demonstrated the company values. Ideally the prior manager will perform the write-up and speak at the calibration. In some cases, however, you may only get to meet individually with the prior manager and

ask questions. Ask your HR representative how this is handled at your company.

4. How do I calibrate a new employee? Most firms will allow a new employee a certain amount of onboarding time. After that stage, the employee should be calibrated as any other employee. If the onboarding period is especially long, you can evaluate the employee on their performance against onboarding goals. If you don't feel like you have enough information to calibrate someone, discuss with your manager and your HR representative on how that employee should be calibrated.

Questions to review after Reading the Chapter

1. Do you know where the job guidelines are for your employees' positions? What about for your management position?
2. What part of the calibration process provokes the most concern? What aspect do you feel least prepared for?
3. Who can you discuss your team's calibration with before starting this process? Your manager, mentor, or HR? Set up time now to meet with these individuals.

Questions to review after your first calibration

1. Did you have an accurate picture of the ideal employee for each role and level?
2. Did you paint an accurate picture of your employees? Have you measured their performance against goals and how they accomplished those goals?
3. As you listened to other managers, did you speak up when your expectations of a role differed? Why did you have differences of opinions? Is that difference documented?
4. How did you change your evaluation of your team? Are there any employees you are still unsure about? Who can you meet with to gain clarity?
5. For new employees, did their gaps and strengths align to what you perceived in their interview?

Questions to review after a several calibrations

1. What patterns in your own preparation are you noticing? What do you do well? What are you consistently forgetting?
2. What patterns in your evaluation are you noticing? Are you always over- or under-evaluating certain company values? How can you adjust your mental bar for those values? How will you communicate that to your employees?
3. What would you change in your company's calibration process? Is it efficient? How

could you spend less time in calibration and still achieve the same result? How could you achieve a better result with the same amount of time? Send an email or meet with your HR representative to discuss your suggestions.

14 - Performance Evaluations

Now that you have completed the employee calibration it is time for the performance evaluation. Performance evaluations are way to reflect on an employee's accomplishments over the past months. Performance evaluations can be thought of as a comparative exercise. You are comparing the employee against an ideal employee. This mythical employee is one that executed all their goals and did so in a manner that reflects the values of the company. Employees are human and will outperform and underperform against goals and values.

What is success?

A successful performance evaluation is one in which the employee's performance is documented and communicated to the employee. There are many things that a performance evaluation is not:

1. **Negotiation** – New managers often get into the trap of negotiation a performance evaluation. Don't do this. As the manager, you must have the confidence to effectively measure the employee against a set of goals and values.
2. **Career Discussion** – Career discussions should be part of a separate conversation. A performance evaluation is a look backward. A career discussion is a look forward.

3. **Excuses** – The performance evaluation is not a time for excuses or discussions on why results weren't achieved. The reasons for the performance against goals and values are important grounding for moving forward, but can be distracting when evaluating end results against goals and values. Be cautious if a performance review spirals into why results are hit or not. A post-mortem evaluation is important but should be handled in a separate conversation. Ideally that conversation should be built into the project and not held during annual review.

When do you do evaluate performance? Companies often have their own timeline for performance reviews. They should be held quickly after the completion of a performance time range. While there may be delays in aligning performance expectations across teams, it is important to provide feedback to employees as quickly as possible after the time period closes. For example, if your review time window is Jan 1 – Dec 31st, a performance review should occur in early January. Waiting until June means your employees are left hanging for 6 months questioning their performance.

Preparing for a Performance Evaluation
In preparation for a performance evaluation you need to evaluate an employee on what they accomplished (goals) and how they

accomplished them (values). Companies may differ on how they rank these two topics in terms of importance, but both should be evaluated in the review.

In the goals section of a performance review, you must capture what goals were achieved and when. Ideally you have been tracking goal performance throughout the year and have this already documented. If not, you will need to spend time re-creating what was delivered and when it was delivered. No need to go into the why at this stage; just write out the facts.

It often helps to have an employee write a self-review before you write their review. Doing so allows you to farm out the documentation of the specific metrics/dates to the employee. More importantly it provides a manager with a pre-read of what the employees point of view is on his or her own performance. In what areas does their evaluation align with your thoughts? Where do you disagree? Read through your employee's evaluation, but limit the impact of the employee's own sentiment in your review. Employees have various degrees of self-worth or self-promotion. Be cautious in interpreting that self-worth/self-promotion to be anything other than differences in cultures or individuals. You are looking at the self-review for alignment of facts.

To prepare the values section of a performance review, gather examples and feedback from peers and partners. Again, ideally you have been doing this throughout the year. If not, you may need to spend time meeting with others to capture this information. Firms often have HR tools that facilitate this feedback gathering. Individuals have their own bias and way of viewing values. Balance how you interpret and use all partner and peer feedback. Blindly adding in a quote from a partner without your own personal understanding of the situation is a recipe for trouble.

My own experience with partner and peer feedback is that it falls into three buckets:

- 5-10% negative feedback – Relatively few people will write truly negative feedback about another person. If you see multiple negative reviews on a company value it is very likely that the employee has a gap in that value.
- 20-30% positive – The effort to craft a positive example is time consuming for a partner or peer. Therefore, treat positive feedback as a sign of something exceptional. Multiple positive reviews on a company value is a sign that your employee is excelling in that area.
- 60% neutral – Most of the time you will get either no feedback or neutral feedback on a company value. This is normal. This tells you that the employee is performing within the norm and that they have not

made an impression on partner or peers. No corrective action is required.

Ultimately, providing strong feedback (one way or another) takes time. An employee's performance must be significantly different than the expectation for a partner or peer to invest the time to craft a well-written feedback.

Writing a Performance Evaluation

Writing a performance evaluation is a significant investment of time for a manager. To make the most of your time, think back on how you have been most productive when writing a paper or preparing a presentation. This may mean blocking out time on your calendar that is uninterrupted. It may mean physically going to a new location. Many experienced managers I know take a few days off from work and sequester themselves with no email to write performance evaluations.

Below is a simple framework for writing an evaluation.

1. **Who/When/etc.** - At the beginning of the document state who the performance evaluation is for, what time period it covers, who is writing the evaluation, etc. It's important to set the context for the document.
2. **Statement of Goal(s)** – State the goals as defined in your goals document. It's important to remind you and the employee

what the goals were for the time period on which they are being evaluated.

3. **Elaboration of Goal** – Be sure to explain the goal fully. This is an important step when you consider that performance evaluations will be used for years in the future when the employee transfers or has a new manager. This step is often overlooked to the determent of future managers. In this section describe in detail the context of the goal. Why was the goal important? What partners were involved? How did the goal help customers, the business, or the team? Place yourself in the shoes of a future manager; while they may know some about the business they may not know anything about the specific goal.

4. **Performance against Goal(s)** – State the metric or deliverable and when it was accomplished. This is often the easiest part of the performance evaluation. Just describe what was performed. Did that performance met or exceed the goal as stated? No need to get into why details at this point; just state the reality.

5. **Strength Values** – In this section you will lay out in what company values the employee is performing above expectations. You must state the value, elaborate on the expectation of performance against that value, and then what the performance was against that

expectation. In this section, use specific examples. While goals are by definition a "did this happen or not" based framework, values rely on human judgment. The bar is less clear for how values are measured, so it is essential to provide examples of the specific way an employee addressed a situation. Again, be cautious in going down why the employee addressed the situation a specific way. Just state the facts of the situation and what was observed.

6. **Improvement Value** – In this section you will lay out for what company values the employee missed the mark. Here it is important to document the specifics of the situation. This area is often where there is the most confusion. Be sure you spend time on all aspects of the miss. Provide additional clarity on the value itself. How do you interpret the value? Additionally, provide detail on the situation. What was your experience during the situation? It can be very tempting for an employee to put their gap against expectation on you as their manager or their peers. As we all know, everyone experiences a situation differently and therefore the employee may think that you or a peer was in the wrong. Do not be led into this trap. Capture multiple examples in the preparation of review and be firm in your language. If several individuals provide the same feedback and/or if your personal

experience is aligned, it is the team
member that needs to improve.

The length of the document will likely vary based
on the level of the employee and the complexity
of their role. Balance the length of the document
for the time you have in reviewing it with the
employee. A 3-5 page document can usually be
reviewed in 60-90 minutes.

Performance Evaluation Meeting

The performance evaluation meeting is an
essential step for managers and employees. It is
important to understand how your employees
process information. It may be beneficial to send
the performance evaluation ahead of time to
allow for more time to read and process. Another
way is to have two meetings. At the first meeting
you present the information, without feedback
from or discussion with the employee. The
second meeting allows the employee to ask
questions and probe deeper on the evaluation.
These techniques should be balanced with your
company's culture and how information is
provided and consumed.

Performance evaluations can be fraught with
emotional intensity. A team member likely
gauges their self-worth against the evaluation.
Pay or recognition may also be at stake. It is
important that you, prepare yourself for that
emotion. How do you get yourself in a state that
you can be the voice of reason during the
review? Block time before and after the meeting

to prepare yourself for the discussion. Think through how you best respond to questions. Some managers may need more or less preparation. Ask yourself what questions may come up? Where in the document do you think the team member will disagree? How will they react to certain section?

In the meeting itself, I start by giving the document to the employee to read. I ask them to read the document all the way through and let them know that we will address each section separately. For each section I ask for their feedback. Remember, that the employee does not have to agree with the performance review. Managers may get caught in the trap of pushing for agreement. If after a conversation, you and employee do not agree, that is ok. The performance evaluation relies on you, the manager, to act on behalf of the company in stating the employee's performance. The review is the company's point of view on the employee.

As you walk through the document the employee may point out factual inaccuracies. If you agree with these points, feel free to edit the document. For example, you may have mistyped a date, or failed to list a partner for a project. If you feel the employee disagrees with an area you believe is accurate, probe to understand their perspective, but remember that you are under no obligation to change your position.

After reviewing the document there is likely a repository of reviews. Upload the review. Often times there is a way for an employee to acknowledge the receipt of the review. This is not the employee agreeing to the review content, just that a performance review was held.

Formal Rebuttals

Before performing a performance review, be sure you understand from HR what processes are in place for an employee to provide a formal rebuttal to his or her review. In some firms this may be an online process where an employee can provide their own self-review. In others, it may be an escalation to a senior manager or HR. Be aware of the process and offer it to the employee if you arrive at an impasse.

FAQs

1. This employee was recently transferred to me, how should I write their review?
   You should request that their prior manager write and perform the review. If that doesn't work, try to meet with the prior manager to gather any feedback. If the prior manager has left the firm speak with their peers, skip level managers, and internal customers to gain some directional insight.

2. When do I discuss their pay?
   Pay is frequently discussed at the same time of the review. However, pay is a very

emotional issue. If possible try to decouple the performance evaluation from the pay discussion. I have seen it work where the pay is discussed first, which gives the employee a chance to anchor themselves. At that point performance is discussed. Getting the pay out of the way can open the employee up to hear about their performance. Another way is to separate them across days or weeks. Have a performance review and then a month later have the pay discussion.

3. This isn't how my company does reviews. Compensation and performance evaluations are going through a significant evolution. The rank and yank model pioneered by Jack Welch has fallen out of favor. Firms are beginning to try new models. Meet with HR, your manager, and your mentor to understand how your firm performs evaluations.

Questions to review after reading the chapter?
1. When was your last review? Did you feel the review was productive? What were you expecting to get out the conversation? Where those needs met?
2. What format was the document written in? How was the conversation handled?

Questions to review after your first
evaluation?
1. Was the review successful? What did the
    employee get out the conversation? What
    did you get out the conversation?
2. How was the employee's body language?
    Did they react the way you expected them
    to? In my experience, I try to forecast what
    phrases or section will evoke reactions,
    but I am often proven wrong.
3. What questions did the employee have?
    Were you able to address them?
4. What will you change before your next
    evaluation? It's important to be deliberate
    about iterating how you approach
    performance evaluations. Don't be afraid
    to try various techniques.

15 - Managing Out

Managing an employee out of the company is often the most difficult task a manager needs to accomplish. It can be emotionally challenging for both you and the employee. Understanding the process and your responsibility within that process can minimize the burden this difficult task places on you.

As with many performance processes, managing an employee out requires a deep partnership with your HR representative. Laws and policies vary dramatically by company and geographic locale. Before beginning the process of managing an employee out, be sure you fully understand the policies of your firm and any applicable laws that you may be required to follow.

What is success?

Success is the termination of an employee following all policies and laws. One way to think about success beyond the termination is to consider how that headcount could be better utilized by the business. If the needs of the business and the employee skills are not aligned, it is the manager's responsibility to fill that resource with an individual who better fits that need. Another way to consider managing out is that rather than termination, it may become a transfer. There may be another role within the company for your employee where they will be successful. Keeping them in a role where they are unsuccessful limits them professional and personally.

When do you do it?

Persistent under-delivering of goals or the inability to meet expectations of values means it time to begin the termination process. New managers often spend too much time in performance management hoping to fix an employee, and fail to move to the managing out process.

There are also times when the role the employee is performing is no longer necessary. The business has evolved or the employee has solved the problem they were brought on to tackle. In these cases, you may need to move the employee out of their role. Often the employee will recognize this and will be more open to having a conversation about finding another opportunity.

How do you do it?

During your periodic review of your employee's performance against goals, or feedback from partners and peers, you may come to understand the employee is not meeting expectations of goals or following company values. It is your responsibility as a manager to hold employees accountable to those goals and values. You should begin the managing out process when a pattern has been identified. While people do make mistakes, consistent failure to meet goals or uphold values means it is likely a misalignment between the employee and role.

Once the gap is identified you should discuss the gap with the employee. Often times the gap exists due to misunderstanding of the expectations for the employee. A specific discussion on where the bar is set and how the employee is missing the bar can often rectify the situation.

If after an initial discussion, the pattern continues it is time to put in place a more formal documentation of what success is, how the employee is failing to meet that bar, and an explicit timeline for meeting that expectation. This document can be called different names, for example: "Performance Improvement Plan" or "Performance Management Plan". A well-crafted improvement plan will provide clarity of expectations for the employee. At the end of a specified time period a well-crafted improvement plan will lead to an easier conversation of the employee's performance. You are looking for an explicit line on performance. Vague terms, lack of deadlines, lack of measurement, etc. are all failures within a performance improvement plan.

It is important to note that even though the performance improvement plan is called a plan it does not include the steps to accomplish the goals. The accountability for delivering against goals must be put onto the employee. If the plan is a series of explicit actions to take the employee may just check the box and perform the actions without accomplishing the goals. The manager must set the end state, while the employee needs to set the steps to accomplish the end state.

When presenting the performance improvement plan it is important that you gain buy-in from the employee on what the goal is and date for delivering that goal. An employee may feel the goal is unattainable, or unrealistic. While that feeling may exist, you must maintain that bar for the employee. The company pays the employee for a set of goals and the employee must meet those goals to maintain employment.

It is recommended to explicitly discuss the employee's progress against the improvement plan on a weekly basis. This likely requires an added investment in time with the employee. At the end of the improvement plan period a formal review (similar to a performance review) should be performed. Provide a formal documentation of results against the stated goals. It should be clear, at this point if the employee should be terminated or if their performance has improved to a place where they can move off the performance plan. If you plan to terminate, arrange a pre-meeting with your HR representative to understand your company's policies and laws on termination.

The termination meeting is often a difficult conversation. Similar to a performance review give your self-time and space to prepare and decompress after the conversation. Employee's will have strong emotions during this conversation. Role playing the conversation with your mentor or HR partner can help you prepare for different situations. You may need HR or more senior managers to be in the room with you to hold the conversation. I strongly encourage you to take on the challenge of leading the conversation. While incredibly difficult, it will build your confidence the next time the situation arises. It will never be easy to manage an employee out, it can become less stressful.

FAQs
1. I've invested a lot of time in this employee; I want to see them succeed.
This is the sunk cost fallacy. You've put in time and effort. Having to manage someone out that you have invested in can feel like a failure of you as a manager. Better to move someone out that you have invested in than continue to invest in someone who will not be successful.

2. If I just give them one more chance I think they can be successful.
This only works if there was something about their first chance that was wrong. Did you set the wrong goals? Was the

timeline too aggressive? If you created a fair and clear improvement plan and they didn't meet it, don't bet that they will meet the next one.

3. They met they goals I set but I just don't see them being successful long term.
   You are stating that you don't believe the performance improvement plan was at the level required to work in the role. That is a failure of the improvement plan, not the employee. It can be effective to build goals in performance improvement plans that show sustained performance. Not just one project or one meeting, but a series of projects or a series of decisions. This can give both sides of the relationship adequate information to understand if the employee will be successful.

4. I want to get rid of my bad employees and keep my good employees.
   I cringe when managers talk about their employees as bad or good. Employees are people with varying skills, abilities and experiences. They are each unique. A categorization of "bad" or "good" is laziness on the manager's side. You are accountable for fully and deeply understanding each employee's strengths and weaknesses.

Questions to review after reading the chapter

1. Do you have an employee that is consistently missing their goals? Is there an employee that is struggling to demonstrate the company's values? Why haven't you started to manage them out?

2. Have you been managed out? If not, try to imagine that situation. What did you feel? What were your concerns? What needs did you have? What stages of emotions did you move through?

3. Have you ever had a peer or partner that was underperforming and the manager didn't remove them? Why do you think they were able to stick around? How did it make you feel? What impact did it have on the business? On that employee? On their manager?

4. Have you seen someone be managed out and find a new role? How did they go about finding that role? How did you help find that position? Did their prior manager assist?

Questions to review after having to manage someone out

1. What went well in the process? Would you change anything about how you approached managing the next person out?

2. What are your emotions now? How did they change as you went through the process?

3. What can you do differently to prevent an employee from getting to this stage?

16 - Motivation

There are numerous theories on the science of motivation. To get yourself or others to act or change is a difficult and complex skill. This chapter highlights motivational factors and how to implement them with your employees.

What is success?

An engaged and motivated team is one in which the employees are eager and excited to come to work every day. They feel appreciated by you and the company. They see tangible signs that they are being recognized and rewarded at a level that motivates them to accomplish their goals.

When do you do it?

Motivation is an ongoing task. Each interaction you have with an employee is an opportunity to motivate or de-motivate them. Every meeting, 1:1, and presentation can offer motivation for your team.

How do you do it?

One way to think of motivation is a gas tank. Each employee has a tank that they draw upon for motivation. Even you have an internal tank that you use. Each activity performed throughout the day fills or empties this tank. Some tasks have a relatively neutral effect on the tank. They may slightly fill or slightly empty the tank. However, some tasks can dramatically fill or empty the tank. Understanding what items fill and empty your employees' tanks is a critical role of a manager.

I bucket items that can increase or decrease their motivational tank into three areas:

1. **Motivational** – Motivational items are actions you can take with an employee that fill up their tank. Take yourself as an example, in the last week what did you do at work that got you excited to come back the next day? Was it accomplishing a goal? Was it a kind word from a manager? Was it a monetary bonus? Was it being highlighted in front of others? Many managers don't understand their own motivational items, much less their employees.

2. **Fair Pay** – This area is often overlooked. Most employees have expectations that won't motivate or demotivate them unless they feel there are being taken advantage of. Often this arises in promotions or compensation. While most people like to be paid, employees understand that not everyone can make the CEO's salary. But they do want to know that they are being paid fairly. Fair pay won't necessarily motivate them, but unfair pay can be a huge de-motivational factor. Another example is scheduling. Again, employees may not be de-motivated about working a weekend shift, if they feel they were assigned it fairly.

3. **Demotivational** – Demotivational items are those that explicitly draw down an employee's tank. Confusion on their role, what success is, being berated, or mocked in front of others are all demotivational factors. It is your job as a manager to not only prevent and stop the clear demotivational items, but also understand the hidden de-motivational factors. These differ from person to person.

As a manager, it is your role to identify the buckets of motivational, fair play, and demotivational factors that each of your employee holds. This can be a difficult task as employees are often not self-aware enough to identify these factors on their own.

To help employees identify items that motivate or demotivate them walk through hypothetical options for recognition and reward. For example: Would they rather get praised in front of the team or in private? Would they rather get a $10 gift card or an email telling everyone how well they did? Walk through some common ways of recognizing individuals at your company and see what resonates with each employee.

To identify what demotivates them talk to them about when they have been demotivated in other roles or in school? What was the situation? What caused them to be unhappy?

Finally work towards a relationship in which the employee is encouraged to identify what behaviors you did that motivated them or demotivated them. Take that feedback seriously and modify your behavior. Often the motivational item will differ from how you like recognition and reward. Use the employee's commentary to adjust how you are motivating them.

FAQs

1. I don't have a budget for gifts or rewards. Remember that not all employees are motivated by financial means. Often employees will respond well to other forms of recognition.

2. But I already recognized them via gift card/recognition/pay increase/pat on the back.
   As a manager, you will have to perform a variety of recognition techniques. You are never done motivating your team. Always be looking for new ways to reward and recognize your employees. You will need to lead a variety of activities to cover your entire team and keep them engaged.

Questions to review after reading the chapter

1. What motivates you? When was the last day you came to office early because you were excited about your day?
2. When have you felt that you were being treated unfairly? How did you address that situation? How did your manager/leadership respond?

3. What demotivates you about being a manager? What is the least fun part of your day? How can you address that de-motivator?
4. Make a list for each person on your team about what excites them and what de-motivates them. Can you do it from memory? If not use your next 1:1 to discuss this with them. It may take several rounds.

17 - Conclusion

My sincerest hope for you is to take these techniques and apply your own ideas and frameworks. These techniques are by no mean set in stone. The tools and skills outlined here are just the starting point of becoming a great manager; they are not the end.

Transitioning from an individual contributor to a manager is one of the most difficult professional transitions you will experience. Take time to invest in yourself. Have you set up your support network? Do you have a mentor? Do you have a set of peers you can discuss these techniques? Keep those relationships going, they will be valuable not just for this transition, but throughout your career.

Remember to come back and review the questions after you have practiced each technique a few times. Reflection is a proven technique for adult learners.

Finally, my virtual door is always open. Please visit ManagmentMentor.com to learn more about upcoming seminars and resources.

Typos
Pg 8 - italicize
Pg 10 - capitalization
Pg 47 - missing plural
Pg 49 - candidate's - missing possessive
Pg 57 0 instead of (?) possessive

Pg 82 - "while"

Made in the USA
San Bernardino, CA
13 November 2017